copy A

The Organization from Within

The ORGANIZATION from WITHIN

A Comparative Study of Social Institutions based on a Sociotherapeutic Approach

CYRIL SOFER

TAVISTOCK PUBLICATIONS

First published in 1961
by Tavistock Publications (1959) *Limited*
11 *New Fetter Lane, London, E.C.*4
and printed in Great Britain
in 11 *point Times by*
Taylor Garnett Evans & Company
London and Watford

CONTENTS

ACKNOWLEDGEMENTS

IT WILL be clear to readers that I have a central debt to the members of the three organizations – the Davidson Company, the James Division and Research Unit, the Helmsley Technical College – who invited me to work with them and subsequently agreed to the publication of descriptions of our joint work. My thanks are due also to my colleagues at the Tavistock Institute of Human Relations: Dr. E. J. Miller, who joined me at a crucial stage of the Davidson project; Mr. G. J. Hutton (now of the University of Edinburgh Social Sciences Research Centre), who worked with me throughout the Helmsley study; and Dr. A. T. M. Wilson (now of Personnel Division, Unilever), who was in overall charge of that project. On several occasions during the Davidson and Helmsley studies my colleague Mr. Harold Bridger helped me to see my way more clearly through the human tangles in which I was so deeply involved.

Professor Meyer Fortes of Cambridge and Professor Irving Janis of Yale stimulated me into recording the studies in detail, explaining the considerations that guided my advice and actions, and attempting generalizations that would enable other social scientists to share something of my experience.

In preparing the final manuscript I have had invaluable help from comments on earlier drafts by Dr. Marie Jahoda of Brunel College of Technology, Professor Irving Janis, Professor Everett Hughes of the University of Chicago, Dr. A. T. M. Wilson, and Dr. E. J. Miller. Mr. E. L. Trist, Chairman of the Management Committee of the Tavistock Institute, and Mr. A. K. Rice, Deputy Chairman, made many constructive suggestions throughout the period of writing and re-writing, and contributed significantly to the final form of the book. Mr. Rice was also kind enough to prepare the final versions of the diagrams. Mr. Stephen Cang and Miss Dorothy Rennison carefully read proofs, suggested changes of language, and drew attention to inconsistencies. Mr. D. W. Langridge prepared the index.

Mrs. Irene Yates managed to retain active interest in the book through innumerable alterations and what seemed to be endless re-typing.

D. W. LANGRIDGE

INTRODUCTION

THIS book is concerned with organizational behaviour. It deals with events within organizations attempting changes in their behaviour, or trying to overcome difficulties that are reducing their capacity to achieve their objectives.

The book is in two parts. Chapters 1, 2, and 3 consist of descriptions of three projects I have undertaken during the past six years in a combined research and advisory role as a staff member of the Tavistock Institute of Human Relations. The first project described was undertaken with an industrial organization, the second with a medical research unit, and the third with an educational establishment. Pseudonyms have been used throughout.

Each study is in narrative form. It begins at the point where I was asked to work with the organization. It presents the emerging data and my growing understanding in more or less the same order and in the same uneven way that I acquired them. I report facts and opinions as they swam into my ken rather than in the form of a predigested research project. I have done this to make it possible for the reader to share something of my experience in coming to understand each situation; to learn something of the atmosphere in which I worked, and of the way I felt at the time about my 'clients' and they about me; and to appreciate the processes actually involved when one works in this way. I think that, despite the common elements, the narratives show the tremendous amount that depends on the individual research worker, the scope for great personal variation in the way this role is taken, and also something of the extent to which the active, clinical-operational part of the role depends on a set of skills which are as yet incompletely shared property among social scientists.

I hope that after studying the three narratives the reader

will feel that he has deepened his understanding of how organizations work. Probably the best indicator of this will be the extent to which he feels he is re-experiencing the familiar, to which he feels a sense of *déjà-vu*. If this is the case, I would suggest that it is because I have described an aspect of the universal experience of those who work in large organized groupings.

Although each organization began the relationship with a request for help, it would, I think, be wrong to regard the three cases as studies with a pathological interest rather than a more general one. It is true that they were experiencing severe crises of different kinds, but a closer acquaintance with organizations (or the simpler if more painful process of introspection about one's own experience in organizations) would probably show that practically every organization passes through similar crises at one time or another. In so far as their crises were pathological, I would submit that all organizations exhibit a similar pathology at some time. Indeed, it could be argued that the organizations here described showed an unusual degree of flexibility, sophistication, and 'maturity' in their handling of their crises, as evinced in preparedness to call in an outside specialist in organizational life and to endure somewhat lengthy and painful searches for solutions, rather than to choose the conventional and relatively familiar courses of resignations, dismissals, and so on.

After recounting what happened in the three projects, I distinguish at the beginning of Part II of the book between the two components of the work – therapy and research – and discuss each separately. Chapter 4 categorizes the main types of help given to the client organization, and compares and contrasts such help with that which the psychotherapist attempts to give his patients. A discussion follows on the research opportunities conferred through an approach that includes an advisory component, and on the difficulties and limitations of investigations conducted in this manner.

Chapter 5 describes similarities in the course run by each of the three projects, common elements in methods of work, and the implications which follow for the investigator. The argument is advanced that the double-focused approach (clinical sociology) can provide a basis for the establishment of a profession (social consultancy) within social science, a profession for which a prescribed theoretical and practical preparation can be developed.

In an attempt to illustrate the types of substantive contribution to social theory which I believe studies conducted on the social consultancy model can make, I set out in the final chapter some tentative generalizations about organizational change. This chapter identifies some of the forces tending to maintain (or to change) existing modes of operation; events or situations that precipitate decisions to change; factors that tend to maintain or oppose a change once it is under way; processes that occur during the change within the innovating group, among its colleagues, and between innovators and observers. It goes on to an account of common systems of 'defence' adopted by groups when they fall short of the targets which they set themselves; and to discussions of the functions of various types of intra-organizational conflict, of the special problems for a subgroup in an organization when it is the main innovator, and of the needs of leadership during critical change.

The stream of work of which this book is part has been particularly associated in Britain with the Tavistock Institute of Human Relations. The Institute is a social research, training and advisory body, which was inaugurated in 1946 as the sociological and social psychological division of the Tavistock Clinic (an out-patient centre for psychiatric treatment), and was subsequently separately incorporated as 'an association not for profit' when the Clinic entered the National Health Service. A tradition of work has become established at the Tavistock Clinic and Institute whose general aim is to relate psycho-analysis and medical psychology to the broader social sciences concerned with structured social groups.

Sociotherapeutic and action research studies of the type discussed in this book have been conducted throughout the history of the Institute, alongside other programmes of work that share the same multi-disciplinary tradition but differ from them in both content and intent. The Institute particularly expresses in its sociotherapeutic and action-oriented studies the views that a scientific approach can assist in the understanding of social problems and contribute to their solution; that where the social scientist is willing to help groups to overcome difficulties he can secure access to crucial areas of behaviour from which he would otherwise be barred; that the various social sciences can most effectively be integrated when those trained in them can be engaged together on a common task. Similar assumptions are expressed in much of the social consultancy, action research, group relations training, applied anthropology, and operations research now carried out by other institutions and individual social scientists in the U.S.A., to some extent in Britain, and, increasingly, on the continent of Europe. The Institute still, however, appears to differ from most of these in the extent to which weight is given to the clinical and psychodynamic component in its outlook.

The early social psychological heritage of the Institute was largely derived from Elton Mayo, Kurt Lewin, and the groups associated with them. The foundation for the work of the Institute was laid during the war when psychiatric, social psychological, and sociological knowledge about groups was effectively welded together in such fields as officer selection, resettlement of former prisoners-of-war, and the treatment of psychological casualties in therapeutic communities. Many of those associated with this work had been on the staff of the pre-war Tavistock Clinic. With others drawn in during and after the war they remained associated in the Tavistock Clinic and Institute of Human Relations. A principal factor in the theoretical orientation of this group, both in the sphere of therapy and in research, became the early post-war formulations of W. R. Bion concerning underlying processes of group life.

My own connection with the Institute dates from 1954. My academic training had been in sociology and my research experience in the fields of community study of the behaviour and relationships of working groups within larger social structures. In the work reported in this book I am deeply conscious of the influence on my thinking and behaviour of the ideas of my colleagues, as they have been affected by the history of our institution, by our more recent experiences and theoretical developments, and by the work of other contemporary social scientists. For my own part I feel I must draw special reference to effects on my outlook of the pychological thinking associated with psycho-analysis and the sociological thinking represented by the structural school of British social anthropologists.

PART I

THREE CASE STUDIES

CHAPTER I

AN INDUSTRIAL SETTING

The Davidson Company

PRELIMINARIES

IN February 1958 the Tavistock Institute received a telephone call from Mr. Edward Adams, the home sales manager of Davidson & Sons, a company well known in its field, asking for help in the selection of a senior manager. My colleague Mr. A. K. Rice arranged to pay a preliminary call on the company. He was met by Mr. E. Adams, who told him that the vacancy was for a chief accountant and secretary. Mr. Rice asked what had happened to the former occupant. He was told that the post was a new one which incorporated but was wider than the existing company secretaryship. The present secretary was Mr. Adams's brother-in-law. He was considering emigrating to Australia. Realizing that events of some complexity lay behind the story, Mr. Rice asked whether this did not pose a problem for the Adams family. Mr. Adams confirmed that this was the case.

At this stage they were joined by the managing director, Mr. D. Bruce. He participated in the conversation for a short while, and then asked what it would cost to have the help of the Institute in making the new selection. Mr. Rice said that clearly more was involved than a selection procedure: the situation required some preliminary study and discussion. If they wanted Institute help they should budget in the first instance for the equivalent of, say, a month's consultant time. Mr. Bruce and Mr. Adams said they would think about this and get in touch with Mr. Rice again.

About a month later Mr. Rice was telephoned again by Mr. Adams and asked to begin the work. As he was just about to leave for India, it was agreed that I should go instead.

I was met by the two men previously mentioned and we were joined in the Board room by Mr. Francis Adams, the production manager. They explained that they were all Board members and that the Board further consisted of Mr. H. Cabot, a full-time executive who acted as export sales manager and was also Board chairman,[1] and Mr. Hugh Adams, a part-time member who had formerly been, like themselves, a full-time member and executive. Mr. Bruce and Mr. Cabot were in the middle fifties and Mr. Edward and Mr. Francis Adams in the early thirties.

All five members of the Board were descendants of the original founder of the firm. The younger brother of Mr. E. Adams, Mr. George Adams, was also in the company. It was their sister who had married Mr. Davis, who was the present company secretary and secretary to the Board.

I learned that this was nevertheless a public company with about 500 employees, of whom about 350 were on the production side, the remainder being clerks and representatives. About 40 per cent of the shares were held within the family (though a much smaller proportion was held within the Board), and the managing director was the largest individual shareholder. The majority of the shares were widely dispersed among the public.

They were a family company in more ways than one. In many cases several members of a family unrelated to the Board were members of the firm. Partly owing to long-established family traditions of this type, and partly because of the specialization necessary (or thought necessary) in this trade, staff turnover was very low. Twenty per cent of the employees had been in the company more than twenty-five years and several more than fifty years. Their present organization was as set out in *Figure 1*.

The Board members whom I met told me that they regarded the post which they wanted to fill as necessitated by the greatly

[1] Accordingly, Mr. Cabot was senior to Mr. Bruce so far as Board membership went, but junior to him in the operational management of the company.

FIGURE 1

ORGANIZATION AND PERSONNEL AT SENIOR LEVEL, MARCH 1958

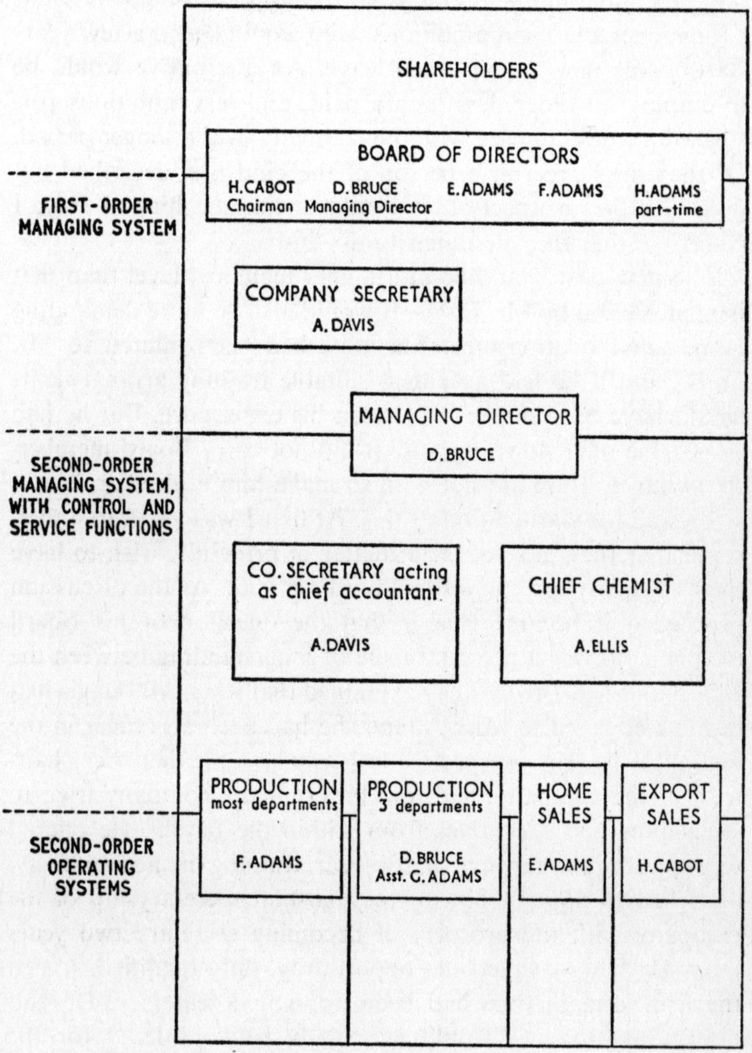

modernized and mechanized accounting procedures which they had just introduced with the help of management consultants. They had considered various possibilities in regard to the new appointment. They could appoint someone new, young, energetic, and ambitious, who would spend a few years starting the new system, then leave. An alternative would be to employ an older, less highly paid, and less ambitious person, who would remain with the company over a longer period. Or they might recruit a person of the kind first described but give him the prospects that would encourage him to stay; I could see that they hesitated to do this.

The new post would be at a higher technical level than that held at present by Mr. Davis. It would also be more demanding in personal relationships. The post had been offered to Mr. Davis, and if he had accepted, suitable training arrangements would have been made to broaden his experience. But he had turned the offer down because it did not carry Board membership with it. They did not wish to make him a director.

I asked for clarification of this. At first I was given to understand that they did not, as a matter of principle, wish to have their company secretary as a Board member. As the discussion proceeded it became clearer that the question of his Board membership was a personal issue of long standing between the Board and Mr. Davis. They explained that when Mr. Davis had become engaged to Miss Adams, he had been an officer in the regular army. His prospective father-in-law, the then vice-chairman of the company, had told him that the company tried to select potential executives from within the family. He offered to support him through a five-year training in accountancy, and then to appoint him to the assistant secretaryship of the company with the prospect of becoming secretary two years later. He had accepted the opportunity, duly qualified, joined the firm, and in time had been appointed secretary. He had understood that he would eventually be considered for the Board. According to those present, the Board as a whole had never been committed to him in this way and members did not feel bound to appoint him a director. He had now given notice that he would leave the company by the end of July and planned to make a new career in Australia.

While they were anxious to have as their new chief accountant someone able to handle considerable technical and managerial responsibility, they were reluctant to hold out to him the prospect of directorship as nobody outside the family had as yet been appointed to the Board.

I suggested that it might be useful for me to have a talk with Mr. Davis. They said he expected this with a view to explaining his present tasks. I needed to check and amplify the description of the situation so far given me, and to ascertain Mr. Davis's feelings about it, in order to improve my understanding of what was motivating his colleagues and himself, and help my estimate of how the various parties were likely to behave if one decision or another was taken.

Mr. Davis told me that he had assumed from the beginning of his career with Davidsons that he would one day join the Board. A vacancy would shortly arise through the retirement of the part-time member. He understood that it was the intention to appoint his younger brother-in-law, Mr. George Adams. It was wrong that a public company should continue so long to be directed by members of one family. Much was antiquated in the company. During the last couple of years it had become increasingly clear to him that he would never get on to the Board. It was for this reason that he wished to leave. He had decided to emigrate to Australia where he had his own family links. There was a senior vacancy at present in the Australian subsidiary of the company. He had expressed an interest in this, but had been turned down for it.

On my return to the directors, I was asked what he had said. I made it plain that it would make my work impossible if I did not carry a confidential professional relationship with individuals side by side with my responsibility to the Board.[1] If I discussed with one person what another told me, the flow of communications to me would dry up. I would be better able to help them as a group by treating individual communications as confidential and letting these contribute towards an overall appreciation that I could share fairly freely.

The meeting ended with an arrangement that the three Board

[1] It will be appreciated that for the same general reasons I have reported in this account only a fraction of the personal interviews mentioned.

members, their absent chairman, and I would meet again a week later, by which time I should have had a chance to assimilate what I had been told, think about various possibilities, and discuss these with my colleagues. We would dine together and then visit their auditor to discuss with him the technical requirements for the new post.

I stayed to lunch after this initial meeting. This was served in the Board room. Those present were the three Board members previously mentioned, Mr. Davis the younger family member, Mr. George Adams, and myself. The meal was eaten in a strained silence.

My staying to lunch was consistent with what is now a not uncommon Institute pattern of associating to a certain degree with 'clients' outside the professional situation as strictly defined. Not to do so would seem unnatural to them and highly discrepant from the ordinary conventions of business relationships to which they are accustomed. There is also the more positive reason that through such association clients are more likely to remain reality-oriented in their perceptions of the social consultant and to regard him simply as another human being who brings a particular type of expertise to bear on their problems.

When we met again the chairman was present. I suggested to the group that we should not proceed to a selection procedure at this stage, but should initiate a series of discussions designed to clarify the needs of the business, the needs of the family, and the relationship between the two; to work out what ways might exist of helping family members without necessarily incurring long-term obligations through employment with the company; and to determine what type of aid, if any, might be given to Mr. Davis in his present position, as one such family member. At the same time, we could work towards a fuller understanding of what the new post would entail and what sort of person should fill it.

I felt that the discussions would elicit facts and feelings relevant to the problems of the company, provide opportunities for fantasies or irrationalities to be tested against realities, and make it possible for the group to achieve a better understanding of the nature of the current situation and of the various possibilities open to them. It was also important to get an apparently divided Board united on some common, objective task.

After a brief discussion, my suggestion was adopted. We arranged a date for our first work on this programme and adjourned to the meeting with the company's auditor.

The meeting with the auditor did not deal with any of these personal or policy issues. The auditor himself was puzzled and sceptical about my role and the value of any contribution the Institute might make. I explained that my main task was to clarify with him and the Board what was involved in the new post and what qualities might be appropriately sought in the person to fill it. It appeared from our subsequent discussion that the new man would have had the foundation laid for him by the management consultants; that he would need previous experience of machine accounting and of budgetary control; and that some qualification in accounting or costs and works accounting would be a minimum requirement, though relevant experience would be more important than the particular qualification held. His post would be creative and influential. He would be responsible for the production of information that might lead to changes in the direction of operations and policy, and should be able to work freely, naturally, and successfully with senior colleagues, feeding them continuous information derived from his own analyses.

THE START OF THE FORMAL WORK

Our next meeting began with a clarification of the qualifications necessary for Board membership. Past policy had been to make appointments to the Board mainly from full-time executives, supplementing their number occasionally from retired former executives. Although the family did not hold a majority of the shares and the family holding was very widely diffused, it had been consistently attempted to recruit potential executives, and therefore Board members, from within the family. Had the time now come to make a change? A share qualification still existed for Board membership and their shares did not come often on the market. If they wanted someone on the Board sufficiently they would have to collect together the required number of shares for him, but it would be quite possible to arrange this.

Members of the Board said that to appoint a Board member – or potential Board member – from outside the family would entail a break with a long-standing tradition. The need to run the company effectively had to be balanced against the wish of the family to retain financial and emotional interest in, and control over, the enterprise that their ancestors had established. They had cherished and developed it. If they ceased to protect themselves in the future as they had done in the past – a practice that had safeguarded the traditions of the business as well – they felt that the business might slip into the control of the families of newcomers who were let in. On the other hand, the current crisis appeared to have strengthened their wish to protect and advance standards in the business and to take decisions in a way less affected by kinship considerations. The two younger Board members seemed especially concerned that they should not be handicapped in the future by the negative components of the heritage with which the present Board, and the managing director and chairman particularly, were now forced to cope. Our discussion showed that doubts about their past tradition were shared by all the full-time Board members, probably to an extent that they had not acknowledged to each other before. While my own estimation of the situation supported their growing feeling that a change was necessary, they seemed reassured at my view that if this involved the liquidation of the existing family and individual interests – as it had to – the liquidation should proceed in progressive stages rather than suddenly and drastically.

The discussion went on to the need seen by the directors for improvement in the quality of management at the level immediately below the departmental headships which Board members themselves occupied. All felt that the present standard of ability here was deficient; this they now began to see as a consequence of recruiting too few young people of outstanding promise. It became clearer to everyone as we went on that the problem of recruiting inadequate middle management was inseparable from the practice of reserving senior appointments and directorships to family members. An additional factor depressing the level of management was, as one director suggested, that family members could not be certain to what extent it was preference which had given them their posts; perhaps they had unwittingly been keeping the standard of recruits low in order to maintain a feeling of unambiguous superiority.

We examined some of the familial and personal implications of present arrangements. While they provided careers for a certain number of young men from the family, did this not involve a risk of eventual damage to profitability and, therefore, to the income of the same people and of their male and female relatives? Was it fair in any case to a family member to recruit him to the company unless he, his relatives, and the senior management were convinced that he was at least as good a prospect for the top posts as the best outside applicants, given the same opportunities? If he was not of that calibre, was it fair to deprive him of the chance of a career elsewhere where he might realize himself? Did the young family members who came into the company do so out of conviction that this was what they most wanted to do? Or were they being influenced by family pressure and expectations? This proved one of the liveliest issues of this and subsequent meetings. Individual members of the senior executive group said repeatedly that they could still not be sure whether they had entered the firm for the right reasons, and to what extent their decisions had been affected by family opinions. They had had to bear the strain of not knowing how far they owed their present positions to their own abilities and how far to their family connections.

I pointed out that it would be possible to avoid some of the problems by arranging vocational counselling for young members of the family before they made up their own minds on these matters. They could also initiate management traineeships, for which both family members and others would be eligible through selection procedures, where their abilities in relation to opportunities open in the company would be scrutinized. This could help to ensure that those family members who entered the firm would themselves feel that they were suitable. The Board would at the same time feel more satisfied that they were safeguarding the managerial standard of the firm and the interests of its shareholders. They would be protecting their successors in senior management from crises of the type that had arisen over Mr. Davis.

As an exploration of the practicability of such a policy, a talk might be sought with Mr. James Adams, a former chairman and managing director, whose grandson was now about fourteen and might be interested in a career with the firm. His parents and he could be asked whether he would be interested in having vocational counselling about his future. This type of help is available through the Tavistock Institute and Clinic. In making this suggestion I had in mind a type of counselling designed to increase the insight of the individual into his own wishes and needs, to advance his knowledge of himself, and to work toward an occupational preference which has a meaning for him and whose immediate and longer-term implications he has weighed against other possibilities. Vocational explorations of this type would help to satisfy the family and the company both that relatives who joined the company did so on reasonably sound 'objective' grounds and that those who did not at least had the benefit of professional help in choosing a career.

We had a further short session on the post of chief accountant and secretary. While the new man would not be appointed to the Board he would be a member of a management committee which it was intended to form from among departmental heads. He would need to be able to distinguish between situations where he was interacting with his colleagues as fellow departmental heads and those where he was interacting with the same people as his directors. As an incoming 'professional' in a position of almost immediate power and influence, and possessing an expertise lacking in his colleagues, he would need exceptional qualities to be able both to stand his ground in debate on policy and procedure, and to refrain from 'controlling' others with his expertise.

As to his prospects, it was agreed that, in the light of the considerations adduced in the earlier discussion, he should be regarded as eligible in the long term for Board membership. This decision, a reversal of what had been originally described to me as the firm's established and preferred practice, was of central significance. It was evident that the group felt driven by the logic of our joint examination of the factors in the situation of Mr. Davis and their relations with him, and by their own discoveries in the course of that analysis, to accept the principle of partial displacement of family members by managers whose claim would reside in personal competence in relation to the needs of the business.

The discussion had produced, therefore, a first explicit recognition, fully shared among the Board members, that a time had come for a break with the existing limiting tradition and that, with the many opportunities available for persons with the qualifications they were seeking, they would be unlikely to secure a first-class person without offering him prospects of the type he could secure elsewhere. At my suggestion, however, the situation was left open for further reflection and discussion. Postponement of the decision allowed people an opportunity to review whether they had considered the full range of possibilities, to make more certain that they were prepared for the implications of their tentative decisions, and to discuss them with their wives and other relatives whose opinion they valued – in other words, to 'work through' the logical and emotional aspects of these problems more fully. It also allowed me to do something similar with my colleagues. For the same general reason, i.e. the necessity of facing the implications of the alternative approaches being considered, I made a practice of drawing attention to the possible negative consequences of each course of action that seemed likely to be chosen. Fuller consideration of this type is designed to increase the likelihood that a decision will not be taken impulsively and that, once taken, it will probably be sustained by the thorough conviction of each of those concerned that it is worth pursuing despite the difficulties that might arise in its execution and the negative consequences that later become apparent.

THE NEW PERSONNEL POLICY

The incipient decisions of the previous discussions were confirmed, though with some qualification and elaboration. Future directors would be appointed mainly, but not necessarily only, from senior managers in the business. Non-family members would be eligible for Board membership. There was no intention, however, to rush this process and it was stipulated that nobody outside the family was likely to be appointed in such a way at this stage.

I was especially concerned to underline the need for caution and slowness because I felt that the family and the company were likely to be upset rather than helped by abrupt change even in a logically desirable direction. Haste would entail the danger of having the form of the change without its real content. Energy and attention could all too easily be diverted from the primary tasks of the enterprise to the secondary task of coping with change.

From time to time appointments would now be made of management trainees, i.e. young men of above average education, intelligence, and promise, who could be given a training that would accelerate their rate of learning and maximize the period over which they might effectively discharge managerial responsibilities. Such traineeships would be open to non-family applicants. Once in the firm, trainees would compete on an equal basis with other employees (and on occasion with external candidates also) for executive vacancies.

Apart from improving the quality of entrants, this would 'objectify' selection and training procedures, satisfy the directors that they were not taking such decisions on kinship and sentimental grounds irrespective of ability, and provide an additional off-centre opportunity for them to learn more about personality and relationships.

Whether or not they were interested in joining the company, young members of the family would be offered help through the Tavistock Institute in exploring their vocational abilities and inclinations and the alternative types of career open to them. In some cases an educational grant from members of the family might be more appropriate than opportunity with the firm. Those who seemed likely prospects for the firm would also be eligible for educational grants – this would be necessary to help them to meet the keener competition with which they would in future be faced. This offer would be limited in scope and duration so as to cover the company and the family over a transitional period.

PRACTICAL STEPS

Mr. Davis, Mr. Francis Adams, and the Australian Vacancy

With a general policy framework now established we were in a position to consider more easily the action to be taken in connection with Mr. Davis. Decisions about his future no longer had to be taken on an *ad hoc* basis.

The Board remained unsympathetic to the prospect of his becoming a director and still proposed to accept the resignation he offered and make a new appointment. He had, however, suffered from the ambiguities and the stress of a situation which had confused personal, business, and familial needs, and would have benefited if he had had available to him at the time he had decided to join the company the type of counselling now contemplated for young family members in similar positions. I suggested therefore that, in the communication the Board now wished to make to him, they should describe the whole of the new policy and offer him a similar opportuntiy of vocational exploration at the expense of the company if he wished it. This could take place at the Tavistock Institute under conditions of professional confidence. If he accepted this opportunity he should see one of my colleagues, as I was the company's adviser and not his own; there would be no communication whatever from his counsellor to the company or to me. These arrangements were worked over and tentatively agreed.

While we had been conducting these discussions, Mr. Davis had asked to be reconsidered for the Australian vacancy. Members of the Board felt that it might be wrong to turn him down out of hand. I suggested a compromise that was agreed: a group selection procedure would be held in July at which Mr. Davis could be offered a candidacy. The Australian general manager would at that time be in the country and could act as one of the selectors; his opinion would obviously carry weight. If Mr. Davis did not wish to accept that candidacy, or was unsuccessful in it, he would be given an *ex gratia* payment equivalent to six months' salary. This could be viewed as compensation for loss of office or as some form of recompense for his disappointment in his expectations within the company. He could use it in a resettlement.

This three-part offer (candidacy for the Australian vacancy, six months' salary if he did not wish this candidacy or if his candidacy was unsuccessful, a counselling opportunity at the Tavistock Institute) was incorporated in a letter drafted there and then. It was arranged that, before being given to Mr. Davis as a formal decision of the Board, this decision should be checked over with the part-time member and finally agreed at a meeting in the next week, which I would attend. It would then be given to Mr. Davis and discussed with him, first by the chairman and the managing director, and then by me.

After this we would proceed to the distinct though related matters of seeing the former chairman about the entry of his grandson to the company and of appointing the chief accountant and secretary.

By the time we next met, the Board had explained their general policy and their intentions regarding Mr. Davis to the part-time director, who, after questions and discussion, had agreed to them. The decision could now be communicated to Mr. Davis. It was to be made clear that the position for which he would be a candidate would be that of assistant general manager, with no commitment about prospects of succeeding the general manager on his expected retirement in a few years' time.

Late in this discussion the production manager, Mr. Francis Adams, said that he might himself be interested in the possibility of going to Australia now as assistant general manager and general manager designate, or of going later as general manager. When Mr. Adams introduced the topic of his interest in Australia as something he wanted to discuss, he made it very clear that he wanted to do so 'here in the group', i.e. in the same way as we had been discussing the other matters. I felt this indicated that members were finding the group method of considering problems constructive. His colleagues did not welcome Mr. Francis Adams's suggestion. They argued that he was more useful here and that the main work to be done in Australia (sales and administration) did not demand his background of production. Mr. Francis Adams said he wished to keep the matter under discussion. Meanwhile, his interest in becoming general manager in Australia underlined the necessity that the candidates who would shortly be competing for the post of assistant general manager should understand that the appointee would not be regarded as the inevitable successor to the general manager.

The Composition of the Board and the Position of Mr. George Adams

The group reverted to the topic of the composition of the Board. If Mr. Davis accepted the offer now to be made to him, this would leave the way clear for the appointment of the younger brother of the sales manager, Mr. George Adams, to the Board. But this might be inconsistent with the new policy of appointment on the grounds of merit irrespective of family connection. On the other hand, it would be unjust for him to have his opportunities jeopardized by the historical accident that such a policy was being adopted just as he was approaching his Board membership. The Board tentatively agreed that rather than make a new appointment they would operate with four full-time directors for a period of time after the part-time director retired. They would tell Mr. George Adams that the question of his membership of the Board was being deferred. He would be offered a new position as assistant manufacturing manager together with membership of a management committee of departmental heads. He would also be offered a series of consultations with me, taking the form first of an appraisal of his potential (which, after clearance with him, would be reportable to the Board), and then going on to counselling sessions designed to aid his development as a manager. There would be no discussion with the Board of this counselling work.

His seniors felt certain that he would be disappointed at the deferment of his Board membership, but they had to balance this against the interests of the company as they now saw them and against the undesirability of adding to their number yet another member who would have no way of knowing whether or not his directorship had been earned. The work with Mr. George Adams should be viewed as part of a general policy. Appraisals would also be conducted with other senior executives below Board level.

I was prepared to handle Mr. George Adams's appraisal and

counselling myself. I would not, in his case, be helping to decide whether he should be given a particular appointment. I saw my task as being much the same as that of the directors, i.e. to bring him on as fast as possible.

Inception of the Management Committee

The management committee would be formed on the appointment of the new chief accountant and secretary. In addition to the present Board and Mr. George Adams, membership would consist of the chief chemist, the assistant manufacturing manager, and, when one was eventually appointed, a personnel and welfare manager. The management committee would consider matters relevant to the day-to-day conduct of the business, and members would exchange information. The committee would implicitly also serve as a training ground for additional Board members and provide opportunities for the existing Board to judge the suitability of their colleagues for Board positions.

I sought at this stage to relate the proposal to form a management committee to existing dining arrangements. At present the Board members and their two relatives, Mr. Davis and Mr. George Adams, met in the Board room for morning coffee, lunch, and tea. If a management committee were to be perceived as the level below the Board that included the other most senior managers, then membership should be coincidental with that of the extended Board group using the Board room for meals. After some discussion of the implications for family privacy of such a move it was agreed that membership of the management committee would automatically carry with it membership of the 'dining club'. This would be a way of communicating through behaviour apparent to anyone that the directors meant what they said – that they were really prepared to share their company privacy with certain senior colleagues chosen on organizational criteria.

Response of Mr. Davis

The chairman and the managing director wrote the agreed

letter to Mr. Davis and discussed its contents with him. Mr. Davis described their new overall policy as enlightened, accepted the place at the selection board for the vacancy in Australia with the alternative of six months' salary if not appointed and said that he would be pleased to use the Tavistock Institute facilities for a vocational exploration. He had been told that he could see me to discuss these matters further and learn more about what would be involved in the vocational exploration. He took this opportunity.

I made it clear to him that the proposed vocational exploration interviews were optional and that he could take this offer up at any stage. I underlined the fact that this would be handled separately by one of my colleagues, who would not discuss either with me or with the Davidson Board what transpired. He might wish to reconsider now, with professional help, why he had gone into secretarial work and the particular vacancy. I told him that many people made a critical reappraisal of their career decisions in the early thirties. After some questions about how long this would take and a further clarification of what would and would not be involved, he asked me to make the necessary arrangements. I did so, communicating the bare circumstances to the colleague concerned.

Meanwhile I continued to build up with the Board descriptions of the posts of chief accountant and secretary, and assistant general manager, Australia, which could be distributed to applicants for these posts when they were advertised. Both descriptions, more especially the former, gave an account of the history of the company, its present structure, and imminent directions of movement, so that applicants would know what sort of situation they would be entering.

Response of Mr. George Adams

The Board confirmed the provisions that had previously been tentatively made for Mr. George Adams. His brother Mr. Francis Adams did not participate in the discussion. As it ended I asked him 'as a brother' how the proposed arrangements looked to him. He described them as 'very fair'. A certain urgency was expressed about the appraisal.

Mr. George Adams had been in the company seven years and now controlled three production departments under the wing of the managing director, who planned later to hand over these departments to Mr. Francis Adams as manufacturing manager. The group seemed to feel responsible for not training Mr. George Adams properly and to wish to make up for this.

Mr. George Adams came to see me, having now had the plans for him communicated to him by the chairman and the managing director. On the new overall policies he said that he was glad about the way things were going: what was happening now should have happened forty years ago. Though he was disappointed about the deferment of his Board membership, he now had precise information about his prospects and the content of his work: it had been confirmed that he was going to have a definite job to do as assistant manufacturing manager and that he would be a member of the management committee (which he had not appreciated before).

He said he had entered the business too abruptly and with too little consideration on all sides. His first preference had been for the regular army. He had been commissioned, had enjoyed his army experience, and retained an active interest in the territorial army. He saw in present events, including the appraisal and counselling sessions, an opportunity to clear up how he was going to get on, and a stimulus to the company to provide him with the training he felt he was not getting. As a member of the family he had not been as free to learn as other newcomers by making mistakes and 'getting among things'.

I told him that the directors wished to make arrangements jointly suitable to him and themselves· and did not see the interests of the company and himself as incompatible.

I saw Mr. George Adams, in all, four times in two months. During this period I reported back to the Board on the question of his development and potential. I thought he needed to retrace certain steps in his training and to fill in gaps. He could certainly be expected to develop his managerial competence, and there was every reason for continuing to bring him along, though it was not yet clear how far he could be expected to go.

Communicating the new Policies

The question had arisen by now of the need to communicate something of the new policy and events to a wider company audience. Speculation could be presumed to be rife, if only because of the extent to which the Board had been closeted with me during the past weeks. The need for some announcement was now urgent. While the chairman intended to report these events at the next annual general meeting, this would not take place until October or November. Unless something was done now (end of April 1958), the external world (in the form of candidates for the post of chief accountant and secretary) would receive, through the job description to go out with the application form, more recent 'news' than the company's own staff. Accordingly, it was decided immediately to convey the same information internally. After some discussion as to who should first be informed, I asked who constituted the most important centres of influence, discussion, and information in the company, and was told that these were certain key long-service managers. It was clear that though they were not necessarily the most senior staff it would be most economic to begin with them, and it was decided to distribute to them the job description of the post of chief accountant and secretary, to invite questions from them, and to indicate to them that they were free to discuss the matter with their colleagues.

We had continued to work on a clarification of what was wanted in the post of assistant general manager, Australia. This had a special importance in view of the candidacy of Mr. Davis for it, the possibility that the assistant general manager might eventually gain the general managership, and Mr. Francis Adams's own interest in the general managership.

Selection of new Chief Accountant

A group selection procedure for the post of chief accountant and secretary was held in May. Each applicant was sent a 1,500-word description of the company, its new personnel policy, the technical requirements of the post, the relationships that would be involved (including the ambiguous nature of some of these), and the rewards and conditions of employment. The procedure included written work designed to show the relative intellectual levels of candidates, and to give the advisers at the procedure (a colleague and myself) some indication of subjective emotional aspects of personality; and a series of events in which candidates were required to compete and co-operate with each other. Some of these included the selectors as participants. The selectors were the four directors.

The two-day event ended with personal interviews, first with the advisers and then with the selectors. These were followed by a Board conference – the last in a series held intermittently through the two-day procedure to allow selectors and advisers to exchange views – at which a final selection was made.

As it turned out, the procedure gave the selectors a further opportunity to reconsider their new policy. The leading candidate of the day was a young accountant with recent management consultancy experience, who could expect to go far, but close behind him was a competent older man who, it appeared, would be content with the post for the rest of his career. The Board chose the younger man, Mr. A. Green, special enthusiasm for his appointment being expressed by the two younger directors despite the fact that this might pose for them in a personal way problems that had been avoided for years by their company.

At the next meeting we began by reviewing the selection of the chief accountant. I took the opportunity to distinguish between the roles played by the Institute advisers and those taken by the company representatives, and to generalize on our proper division of labour from this: I said it was primarily our task to bring information to light and to present alternatives, and primarily theirs to make the decisions. A date had now been fixed for the new chief accountant, Mr. Green, to start. His employment would overlap with that of the former secretary, who was still on the staff and awaiting the Australian selection procedure.

Selection of Assistant General Manager, Australia

We resumed work on the question of the Australian post. At

my suggestion it was agreed that the selection board should consist of the chairman, the managing director, and the general manager of the Australian subsidiary. We needed to avoid the invidious position that would arise if the two younger men, both of them his contemporaries and relatives, sat in judgement on Mr. Davis. The managing director raised the additional question of Mr. Francis Adams's interest in this post. Mr. Francis Adams spoke of his feeling that prospects were generally better abroad, and about the company's lack of a policy in the matter. The managing director said that Mr. Francis Adams was needed at home, and that if he were to go abroad he would be better fitted for South Africa, where it was proposed eventually to start a factory, than for Australia where the needs were mainly commercial and administrative.

I tried to get the group to be more specific about what they wanted and what was troubling them. Eventually I said that I thought Mr. Adams's wish to go and the feelings around the table had something to do with relations between the Board members, with inter-departmental and personal difficulties between Francis and Edward Adams, and with their concern about their relative positions in the future. Eventually a choice would have to be made between them for leadership of the organization; at the moment this was an unresolved issue affecting all deliberations and decisions.

After further discussion it was agreed that the Australian post should be advertised as arranged, that a selection procedure should take place in July, and that we might initiate a study in September of relations between the departments of Mr. Francis Adams (production) and Mr. Edward Adams (sales), after which Mr. Francis Adams could finally decide whether he really wished to go to Australia. Mr. Francis Adams said he was prepared to take the risk that an outstanding appointment would be made that would reduce the need to look further for a prospective general manager.

As in the case of the chief accountant's post, a detailed job description was circulated to all applicants and a group selection procedure was held for a final short-listed number.

It would clearly be a considerable strain for Mr. Davis to compete with external candidates for a post before his directors, and relatives by marriage. They had, as he well knew, to consider the needs of the company, and to ensure that the man selected was at least as good as other aspirants and preferably better. The experience he had gained with the company, and his qualifications and competence, were advantages. On the other hand, tension had been growing in their relations with him. They had to estimate the extent to which the difficulties were determined by the situation in which he had found himself, or were rooted in his personality. To what extent was he benefiting by the counselling he was receiving and likely to continue benefiting in a new work environment? If he were appointed this would help to solve one family problem, but might raise another in regard to Mr. Francis Adams's interest in the appointment.

Towards the end of the procedure it seemed that a candidate other than Mr. Davis was likely to be judged best by the selection board, though his position was less clear cut than that of the chief accountant had been. By the end of the group events this candidate was rated first on performance, with Mr. Davis second. In the final individual interviews, however, first with me and then with the selectors, his stock fell somewhat, though we had made this judgement independently. By contrast, Mr. Davis appeared to have done relatively well. In the interview with the other adviser he presented a balanced view of himself and his personal situation, and showed a dignity and courage about the outcome of the procedure. After a careful discussion with the advisers and a final separate meeting without us, Mr. Davis was appointed.

In order to retain an objectivity of judgement we had arranged that Mr. Davis should be seen by my colleague. He was especially careful in his report on Mr. Davis to describe what the man was like rather than to indicate whether in his view he should be appointed to the post. We felt it essential that the selecting group should bear the full responsibility for the decision. I also wanted to make it clear to the two younger members of the Board, who listened to the selection conference at the end of the day though they did not participate, that we were not 'taking sides' between individuals or factions, i.e. between Mr. Cabot, Mr. Bruce, and Mr. Edward Adams on the one hand, for whom the selection of Mr. Davis might come as a relief because it would mean that a relative was not to be rejected from the business; and Mr. Francis Adams on the other, for whom it would mean the possibility of a door closing in his face.

The new Management Structure

With the appointments of Mr. Davis to the Australian post and of Mr. Green to that of chief accountant and secretary, the new management was now constituted. Mr. Francis Adams was given responsibility for all manufacturing (including the three departments previously under Mr. Bruce). Mr. George Adams was made his assistant. Mr. Fox, a former engineering consultant recently employed in the manufacturing department, was appointed development manager on a level similar to that of other departmental heads, and also reporting directly to the managing director. He was made responsible for introducing new processes, work study, and incentive systems into the manufacturing department. The Board had now been reduced to four full-time senior executives (all relatives). The management committee was formed and consisted of the Board; together with Mr. George Adams, twenty-seven-year-old younger brother of Mr. Edward Adams; Mr. A. Ellis, the chief chemist, an employee of the company of long standing; and Mr. Green and Mr. Fox, the two recently recruited 'professional' managers.

The new arrangements were as shown in *Figure 2*.

A MANAGEMENT DEVELOPMENT PROGRAMME

We then proceeded to plan a management development programme designed to raise the quality of management and improve the competitive capacity of the company. I was invited to a meeting of the newly formed management committee to discuss the initial steps. It was agreed that the company would wish to appoint the best people to posts, irrespective of whether applications were external or internal. Internal candidates should not be overlooked and the best use should be made of the potentialities of existing staff.

FIGURE 2

ORGANIZATION AND PERSONNEL AT SENIOR LEVEL
JULY 1958

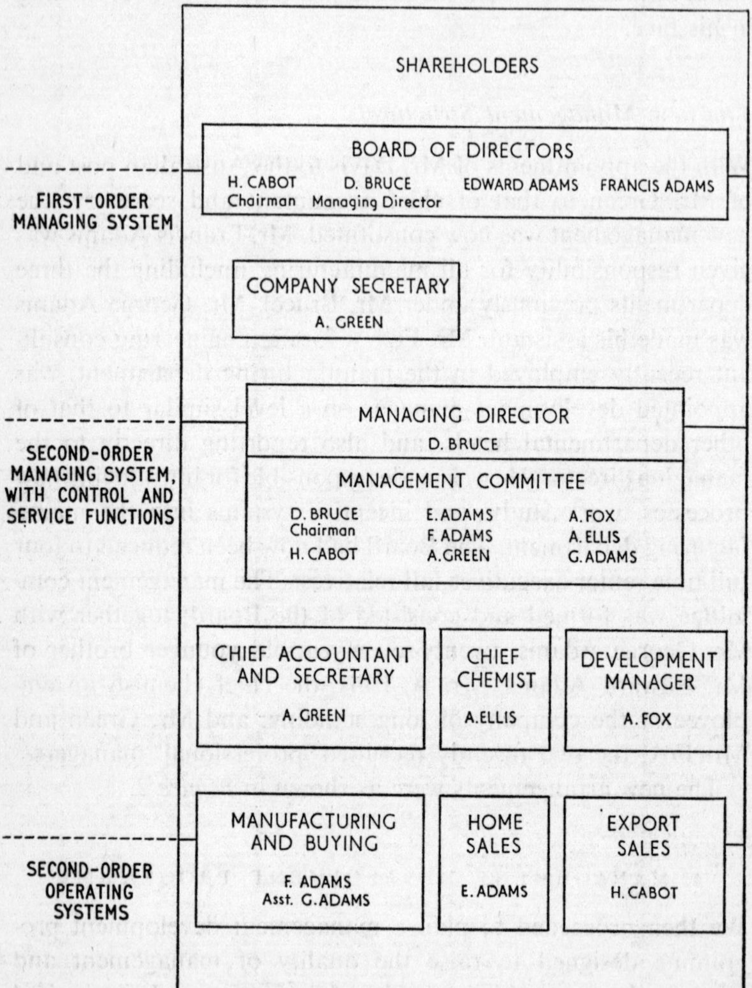

Priority would be given to the appraisal of junior executives between twenty-five and forty years of age. Junior executives would be nominated by members of the management committee, but would participate in the appraisal procedure only if they agreed to do so. No appointments would be made as a direct result of the appraisal procedure. It would be followed by a discussion with each executive of the results and implications of the appraisal, and of the best use he and the company could make of whatever information had emerged.

This would be followed by an appraisal of promising junior employees in a similar manner, men of good educational level, up to the age of twenty-five; they would, at the same time, be considered for formally designated management traineeships. The procedure would help to ascertain the supply of potential managers already within the company. Those designated as trainees would receive special developmental opportunities which would include planned experience of different sides of the business, tutoring by a management committee member, and, where appropriate, external training; this would help to ensure that as many internal staff as possible would be fit to compete for such specific managerial vacancies as would arise.

It was agreed that a description of the management development scheme should be published in the company's weekly newsletter. It was essential that staff should understand the scheme, that young persons outside the ranks of those nominated should appreciate that they would eventually be included in training plans, and that those considered too old for one or other part of the scheme should know that specific vacancies would remain competitive.

As staff would inevitably have questions to raise and suggestions to make about the intentions of senior management, I suggested that representatives of the Board should take a draft description of the scheme to a managers' committee and a foremen's committee (which I now found to exist) to discuss it with them. The chairman and the managing director did this. So far as I could gather from their subsequent account and from the minutes of these meetings, there was a flurry of anxiety and insecurity in both groups, coupled with a feeling that some methods for ensuring objective selections and adequate training were desirable. The foremen's committee seemed at first to dislike the ideas presented, and then proceeded to complain of certain past appointments made on less systematic bases and to work towards the view that something like the approach described might reduce mistakes. Eventually the description of the scheme was published in a special supplement to the weekly company newsletter.

Appraisals of existing Staff

In finalizing arrangements for the appraisal of junior executives, we agreed to discuss each nominee beforehand in the light of past experience of him and a report on him from his departmental head. It was further agreed that it was not the function of the appraisal board to assess the executives' competence in his current post (i.e. the rightness of his appointment). What was being assessed was his capacity to grow with that post or into other, more demanding, posts.

When the appraisal procedure for junior executives was conducted, only one man, a production manager with a science degree, seemed likely to progress to a distinctly more senior level. The others would probably make limited progress within the roles or along the paths already laid down. I suggested that the first man might profit from external training; the others could do with further developmental experience within the business. We agreed on the same day to conduct the planned appraisal procedure for the younger men before deciding whether a new intake was necessary.

It was important that everyone in the company should know that, anxious though the company was to raise the quality of its management, the greatest care would be taken to ensure that internal talent was recognized and developed.

It was agreed at my next meeting with the management committee that we would continue the staff stocktaking by seeing eight young people, to establish how far they were likely to go and how they could be helped. We arranged that each executive seen at the previous appraisal board would now have a discussion of his position and prospects with his line superior and one member of the appraisal board. At the same meeting Mr. Francis Adams requested appraisals of people in supervisory positions in the factory. Many of these, especially the older employees, were of poor quality, and held supervisory positions only nominally in recognition of length of service. A need existed to rationalize their position and decide to what extent future supervisory vacancies could be filled from within the company.

After the appraisal procedure it was decided to designate four members as management trainees; they were young men who, with suitable guidance, might reasonably expect eventually to attain one of the senior sixteen posts in the company. The technical training needs of each trainee would be examined with him, he would be given experience of various sides of the business as opportunity arose, and, with the others, would receive a form of group tutorship with various members of the management committee over a period of two or three years.

Rationalization of Junior Management Structure

At the same time the manufacturing manager told me that the company was trying to bring such persons as senior clerks, and foremen in charge of sales and manufacturing departments, into one structure with a common salary scale and with prospects of promotion from one side of the business to another. Problems had arisen with regard to the relative seniority of the posts involved, the suitability of various people for them, and the salary decisions that needed to be taken. Certain preliminary decisions had been taken, including the demotion of elderly employees with long service. He and the managing director (who telephoned me subsequently with his own second thoughts) were not happy about the way the matter was going, and would like my help. I arranged to attend a meeting with the management committee on this subject, and to bring an anthropologist colleague, Dr. Eric Miller. Dr. Miller had special experience in the organizational field, and would have more time than myself to devote to detailed work with the company if this was required in the following few weeks. At the same time, as I was going to be away over Christmas 1958 and also in May and June 1959, I needed to begin to provide the company with an alternative adviser to myself.

It was agreed that during January Dr. Miller would make brief studies, in collaboration with the manufacturing manager and the sales manager, of a sample of two production posts and two commercial posts. He would describe the tasks of the department involved, the responsibilities of the supervisor, his main relationships with superiors, colleagues, and subordinates, and the technical and psychological demands of the post; and would try to suggest an ordering of the levels of work involved.

While these studies were in progress Dr. Miller and I attended the first meeting of 1959 with the management committee. At this meeting it was decided to try to recruit additional management trainees from outside the company. A short-listed group of applicants would be invited to a group selection procedure designed to appraise their managerial potentialities (alongside any technical qualifications) in relation to opportunities in the company. Successful applicants would receive guided experience in the company's operations before their main fields were determined. They would be advised that this would form part of a wider management development programme, planned and executed in collaboration with the Tavistock Institute, and having special regard to the development of effectiveness in positions of responsibility in organizations.

Start of an internal Training Programme

At the same meeting we considered what training might be given to the junior executives who had participated in the appraisal procedure of October. Dr. Miller and I felt that any form of training should be related as closely as possible to operations. A group of people who had to collaborate in their ordinary work would clearly be most suitable. At Dr. Miller's suggestion it was agreed that the executives in the manufacturing department, with functions relating to production planning and buying, should be brought together into a 'control group' with combined operational and training objectives. Under the new procedures being introduced these men would play a central role in the collation and dissemination of information regarding sales requirements and production estimates and progress. The statement below, which was published in the company's newsletter, summarizes the arrangement:

> In accordance with the need to integrate the different operations of the company, a control group is being formed of those who will be closely concerned with production planning, stock control, costing, and buying under the new form of organization now being completed. This group will consist of Messrs. .... This group will meet fortnightly, at first to gain an understanding of the nature and implications of the new control procedures and the information that will become available on these, and later to receive this information and co-ordinate its actions around it. The manufacturing manager will take the chair. The home sales manager and the chief accountant will attend the first meeting to contribute to the discussion of control functions as now envisaged. With other executives, they will be available for subsequent consultations by the control group as and when necessary.
>
> While the main objective of the control group will be operational it will also have a training component. To assist particularly with this side of its activities a member of the Tavistock Institute of Human Relations will attend meetings of the group for an experimental period.
>
> It is tentatively proposed to form one or two similar operational-cum-training groups on other sides of the business. Their precise form will depend on experience with the control group.

I attended the first four meetings of this group. Mr. F. Adams wondered whether participants would fear that they were being appraised, as this was the situation in which they had met me in the first instance. On my advice he dealt with this explicitly from the Chair. Statements were made by several of the group that 'they co-operated well with colleagues', the implication being that my job was one of smoothing problems over and that I would have no contribution to make so far as they were concerned. My role became clearer when I intervened to make the following points at appropriate stages in the discussion: one should not skate over anxieties, but try to voice them and deal with them; expertise and information should not be used for power purposes by advisers to impress or control executives; people feel nervous and insecure when asked to change to new work procedures.

My impression from the meeting was that people's knowledge of the company and its procedures left much to be desired, and that it would be of benefit to them to discuss these matters with their seniors in the way provided for.

Subsequent meetings continued on the same lines. Mr. F. Adams provided information and led discussions on practical problems, and I made comments designed to draw the group's attention to the processes that ensue when people work together, illustrating from what happened when we met.

I attended four meetings of the group, then stopped, on my initiative, as I felt that I should withdraw from this new internal training event as soon as it seemed to have gained a momentum of its own. My withdrawal at this point proved a misjudgement. I learned later that the series had not proved of either administrative or training value, and had been discontinued. While I could not be sure of the reasons for this failure, my experience with the control group suggested that members were over-vague about their current and proposed functions, that those functions were more clerical in content and level than they were prepared to face, and that my absence after the first phase had reduced their motivation to continue their exploration.

We did not proceed with the plan to constitute similar groups on other sides of the business.

Relations with the Management Committee

Meanwhile, during January and February, Dr. Miller had been conducting his study of supervisory roles. The meetings at which we presented a report on these were marked by tension between Mr. Green and Mr. Fox on the one hand and ourselves on the other. Mr. Green and Mr. Fox, both former advisers to business managements, criticized our descriptions on the grounds that they were of a sociopsychological character which the company could not replicate. They thought it would have been better if we had prepared a simpler model that they could themselves operate on other supervisory posts and a scale that would allow comparison between one post and another. Dr. Miller and I argued that such methods sacrificed understanding for the sake of an attempt at precision that was less likely to help than to mislead. After a long, and partly unresolved, discussion, it was agreed that company members should complete further supervisory job descriptions on their own and rate these by using the described posts as reference points. At the same time they would list any matters of supervisory organization that arose in these descriptions. We would try to help them at a later meeting both with the ratings and with these organizational points.

Lying behind the difficulties and compromises of this meeting was the wish of Mr. Green and Mr. Fox to show that they could handle the technical managerial needs of the company largely on their own. Also, they must inevitably have seen the Institute as only partly committed to 'scientific' management, and have regarded us as over-identified with 'human aspects' of the position of the family group still in charge of the firm.

OVER-EMPHASIS ON STRUCTURAL AND PROCEDURAL ISSUES

Dr. Miller's observations of the ways in which the company was going about its work sharpened in our minds certain issues that were wider than the job evaluations on which he had been engaged. He pointed out that the management committee was functioning as an executive arm rather than an advisory group to the managing director, and that too many people were involved in the decision-making process. His work in the manufacturing department had led him to the opinion that the rapidly growing functions of the development engineer were competing with or limiting those of the line management of the department, rather than providing a service to them. He doubted the functional necessity for the assistant manufacturing manager role filled by Mr. George Adams. He had been a little surprised to find the buying function of the company located in the manufacturing department and being handled by a clerk.

These issues seemed inseparable from the overall problems of the company as I had seen them during the past year. We decided that they should, in the first instance, be broached with the managing director. I asked the managing director accordingly for a special meeting, with himself in the first place, on the subject of overall trends in our work with the company.

We put our view to him that attention was now being diverted from the primary tasks of the company to issues of relatively peripheral importance, such as the precise constitution and procedures to be followed by each management group, the exact rights and duties attached to each management role, and the details of appraisal interviewing and time-tabling. It was evidently easier to work on these matters than on others more painful but also more central.

In the name of participative management, the structure of the company was becoming top heavy and over-elaborate and an uneconomic amount of work was being done on a committee basis. At meetings with us on personnel matters, for instance, all eight members of the management committee were involved, whereas in another company it would be one or two people. Now that the main personnel crises were over and a new policy agreed, this seemed to be the time to return to the immediate commercial interests of the business, and to discourage more distraction from practical management than was necessary.

Apart from diseconomies and distractions, the management committee was functioning less as an advisory group to himself as chief executive than as an informal decision-making body, the consensus of whose opinion was binding on individual members. Was the management committee being used directly to advance the interests of the business or, unwittingly, for the covert purpose of government by committee?

In the ensuing discussion it became abundantly clear that the management committee was attempting to influence individual managers through group pressure, where they should have been commanded by their executive superiors or had views directly communicated to them in colleague-colleague contact. The group situation enabled people to express themselves in general terms or by implication, and made it possible for so much support to grow for a viewpoint, for instance about the way a particular department was run, that the manager in charge had little alternative to conceding that the view was correct and that his actions should follow on it. The functioning of the management committee was only one of several indirect devices being used to avoid potentially difficult personal relations between managers. Another was the mechanized system for keeping sales and production in step – whatever technical advantages the system possessed, it seemed to be a device for avoiding difficulty in the relation between the production and sales managers.

The managing director did not entirely agree about the over-use of committee procedures. He pointed out that they had a beneficial training function as well as being operationally useful. He confirmed, however, that much of what we described was connected with attempts by managers who were related to each other to avoid personal conflict. It was also connected with attempts by the other managers, unrelated to them, to make their point without offending family susceptibilities.

We expressed our opinion that the development function was growing out of proportion to the size of the company. The managing director was concerned about this fact, about the rivalry between this function and line management in the manufacturing department, and about the long-term implications of the emerging competition for eventual company power. A connection existed between the problems observed in the management committee and those within the manufacturing department – in seeking to avoid executive management and the risk of accentuating personal difficulties between themselves, the family members had opened a way for the incoming professionals to build themselves positions of rapidly growing status and influence. One possible effect of this would be to prejudice the prospects of Mr. George Adams, whose current position did not carry the functional importance or confer the prominence available to both the development engineer and the chief accountant.

Mr. Bruce invited me to discuss these matters with the Board. At the Board meeting I made the following points:

(i) The structure was becoming too complex and too fixed.
(ii) Procedures were proliferating. Were these not going beyond the real needs of the company?
(iii) There was a danger of losing sight of individual executive management. There did not seem to be enough person-to-person management. Were people sufficiently held to direct account for what they did or did not do?
(iv) One part of the structure that was becoming out of hand was the department of the development engineer. Was not this function being over-emphasized in a company of this size?
(v) While the development function was being allowed too great a growth, the position of buying seemed to be insufficiently recognized. Should not this work, carried out at present by a junior executive in the manufacturing department, be more centralized, be raised in status, and become the responsibility of a more senior person?
(vi) It would probably be best to clear up some of the existing anomalies in the position of Mr. G. Adams. Unless his role was fully understood to be a specially created and temporary one designed for training purposes, the functions and rights attached to it might gain exaggerated importance and distort the structure further. So far as his personal position was concerned it would probably be desirable to try to advance his potentialities through forms of training and experience that would give him greater scope.

There was not a great deal of reaction to my remarks about the substitution of committee procedures, and structural preoccupations and devices, for executive management. Presumably the Board members were not ready to examine a situation which would confront them with their personal relationships and, in turn, with the implications of these for the future power position within the company.

The significance of the rising position of the development

engineer was noted, but there seemed less wish to take action about this than on the position of Mr. George Adams. It was felt that not enough was being done to help him towards the prospects that had been held out to him. Even though he had not been given Board membership at the time originally envisaged, it remained the intention to bring him along as fast as possible, and to avoid having the recent changes penalize him through the sheer accident of their timing. His brother Edward was especially definite in his request that he should be given a sound training, and have this related to a future post whose functional importance would be obvious to all and in which he could realize himself.

The question of Mr. George Adams's position became linked in the discussion with the need Dr. Miller and I saw to centralize buying and put it under a more senior person than the present man. The suggestion emerged that Mr. George Adams might be groomed to take this post about two years hence, on condition that he first spent six concentrated months each in the production and sales departments, and that some senior person took over the buying in the meantime, and made an appreciation of sources and trends. The most suitable senior person seemed to be Mr. Cabot; it would be possible for him to leave the post of export sales manager. I felt the proposed solution for the future of Mr. George Adams over-neat. Pressure developed for this despite some demurrals evidently connected with reluctance to alter a division of labour between Board members, which had been found workable over the years though not necessarily optimal for the company. The question then arose of what Mr. Cabot would do after building up the buying function and inducting Mr. George Adams. A debate developed about whether a role would exist for a chairman *qua* chairman who could visit customers and 'impress them with the interest of the top of the organization'. Some members of the group lacked the conviction that such a role existed. The meeting did not reach any decision and the issues were left to simmer.

It was clear that the future of Mr. George Adams, though difficult enough to determine, was, of all the questions raised, the least difficult for the Board members to try to work out together. It would have been wrong for me to collude with the Board in the use of devices to avoid difficulties that could in the long run only injure their interests, and I would have felt irresponsible if I had not pointed out the issues as I did. But it seems, on reflection, that they could see no alternative between their present procedural and structural compromises on the one hand, and outright breaches of personal relations among them on the other, and that they were not prepared to have the breaches.

As this was my last formal top-level discussion with the full Board, I cannot report in detail on subsequent events. We were, however, told later of two main consequences. One was that an attempt was made to expand Mr. George Adams's responsibilities with the manufacturing department – he received the benefit of on-the-spot training from a firm of production planning consultants, gained new technical skills, and began to specialize on that side; plans were again being made for him to join the Board in the near future. The second change was that Mr. Cabot took over the buying function; we were told that he was receiving a good deal of satisfaction in it.

VOCATIONAL COUNSELLING FOR YOUNG FAMILY MEMBERS

Meanwhile, work had started in the vocational counselling of young family members, as an inseparable component of the long-term overall policy designed to safeguard and improve the functioning of the firm, while at the same time helping key individuals to determine whether they really wanted to try to join it.

In September 1958 I saw the first boy to whom vocational guidance was offered – a fourteen-year-old grandson of Mr. James Adams, the former chairman and managing director. His parents were under the mistaken impression that anyone who wanted to come to the company now had to be seen by the Tavistock Institute first, i.e. that our responsibility in cases of this type was a selection one. They saw the Institute as the new gatekeeper to the firm's management. I explained at some length the background to the vocational counselling service offered by the Institute, and its objective of helping boys to decide what they really wanted to do. The Davidson firm was happy to consider young relatives for management traineeships if they were sure in their own minds after a period of counselling that this was what they really wanted, and if they were prepared to compete on equal terms with external candidates of the same age group. Both sides had to be sure of what was wanted and what was needed, in view of the subsequent problems that could arise for both the individual and the company – as the past year had so clearly demonstrated.

If the boy decided after due deliberation and the consideration of alternatives that he preferred not to enter the firm, or if the directors decided not to take him, members of the family would be willing to consider some other form of practical help to him in his career. They might, for instance, conceivably contribute towards the cost of a university training.

When greater clarity was achieved in the initial interview the parents became very interested in the prospects opened up by these arrangements and in the long-term benefits that could result for their son. If he went into the company he would have the satisfaction of knowing that the matter had been fully considered by all sides, or he might be helped by the family in some other way more directly to his long-term advantage.

The boy said he was interested in the possibility of entering the company or of a career in some form of engineering. He was uncertain what the latter would offer, and what the precise requirements were. He needed some information as he would have to decide soon in what subjects to specialize after taking his General Certificate of Education Ordinary Level examinations in 1959.

We formed a clearer picture of the objectives of the guidance and what might reasonably be expected from it, and arranged that a series of vocational consultations would take place when the family was ready; these have taken place during 1959 and 1960.

CONTINUING WORK

Since the events reported in this account, contact with the Davidson company has greatly lessened. We have helped the

Davidsons on several occasions with selection and appraisal matters, and in connection with the psychological health of executives. The persons involved have usually been in positions below management committee level, and, by what seems to have been a tacit agreement, neither the company nor we have tried to stimulate more frequent or higher-level meetings. We have not been involved with the Board in top-level policy consideration. On their side, they have presumably preferred to continue with the current equilibrium as long as it could be maintained without dismissals, resignations, or overt and manifest damage to the business. In these circumstances there has not been a significant role for the Institute to play. An additional factor reducing the amount of contact might be inferred to be the wish of the new professional managers to show how much they could contribute to effective organizational functioning. And it must have been seen at the Davidson end that we regarded the protracted discussions that were developing with us over management traineeships, training methods, and so on, as diversions from their central needs (additional commercial effort and fuller rationalization of senior management structure), and that we wished to avoid supporting such diversions.

Nevertheless, our contacts with the company have been sufficient to keep the relationship alive, and to carry with them the communication that the facilities of the Institute remain available if these are again found necessary.

CHAPTER 2

A MEDICAL SETTING

The James Division and Research Unit

PRELIMINARIES

WHILE I was away from London on an assignment a message came from the office of Dr. Andrews that he would like to see me. I was informed that Dr. Andrews was director of a psychiatric research unit newly established within a very large, century-old local mental hospital.

When Dr. Andrews and I met he told me that his unit was supported by an external research-financing organization. A considerable investment had been made and great hopes had been placed on the way in which his unit was set up and the programme that was expected to emerge. It was hoped that the research programme would benefit greatly from a location where abundant and varied clinical material would be available, and where research workers could directly observe phenomena not reproducible elsewhere. Successful collaboration between research scientists and clinical colleagues could lead to a better appreciation of the role of both, and to the development of therapeutic and research techniques especially applicable to large mental health populations.

The hospital had several 'divisions' (sets of wards with their own staff), and his unit had been established within one of these. It had seemed important from the outset to integrate the research operation as closely as possible with the life of the hospital, and to ensure that the clinical setting of the studies was roughly representative of the hospital population and operation. Accordingly, rather than attach the research unit to one of the newer divisions, it had been attached to the James Division which was one of the older hospital units. Funds from the external financing sponsors had, however, been used to adapt part of the building for up-to-date laboratory and experimental accommodation, and to augment the nursing services at the disposal of the division, as well as to make appointments of research physicians, and laboratory scientists and technicians.

In some respects a promising start had been made. At the same time certain difficulties were arising between the James Division and the central administration of the hospital, between the James and other divisions, and within the James Division itself.

Dr. Andrews knew the Tavistock Institute had conducted several organizational studies that included an advisory component, and wanted me to look over the unit to see if there was anything helpful I could say or do about it.

He invited me to come to the hospital as soon as possible and meet his staff. He suggested that I discuss with them the way the unit was going, and tell him afterwards what I thought. I said I would not like to see his people without him, but would be happy to talk with him and his colleagues about their unit. He agreed to this alternative suggestion, saying I was the person who had expertise in this area. We arranged an appointment.

When I arrived I asked for Dr. Andrews. I was told that I was expected by Dr. Butler, consultant in charge of the James Division. Dr. Butler began by asking what he could do to help me. I explained that I was at the hospital at the invitation of Dr. Andrews, not on my own initiative, and that I understood that I had been asked to come because it was hoped that I would be able to provide some form of help. We were unable to pursue the discussion as he was immediately called away.

I was introduced instead to two doctors, Dr. Callendor and Dr. Dailey, who showed me round the eight wards within the division and described to me a piece of research, newly begun, on which they were jointly engaged; this involved a form of case allocation among nurses as well as physical treatments.

At the end of the afternoon I saw Dr. Andrews for a few minutes, in the company of Dr. Callendor. He asked me to return on the following Monday.

The inception of these contacts seemed to me to be unfavourable for the work it was proposed I should do. I therefore wrote to Dr. Andrews as soon as I returned to my office to say that if I was to do any useful work with him and his colleagues it would be necessary for me to meet Dr. Butler and himself together at my next visit so that we could clarify why I was there and what I was expected to do. An announcement would also need to be made to the rest of the staff.

On my arrival, however, I found that Dr. Andrews was not present. I was met instead by Dr. Callendor. He invited me to accompany him to a staff meeting. I demurred on the grounds that it might be confusing to the staff if I was introduced as a visitor and my role changed to one of research worker or consultant. I asked to see Dr. Butler and we went in to him together. Dr. Callendor said that he had invited me to attend the staff meeting. Dr. Butler very properly reacted against this idea, for reasons which (though he did not yet know this) were very similar to my own. He went on to say that we should have a meeting with Dr. Andrews before I began any observing or any other type of work, and to warn me against the dangers of beginning research without adequate preparation of those who would be encountered in the field. Dr. Callendor explained that it had been his idea, not mine, that I should attend the meeting, and that I had said I did not think it would be right and had asked instead to see Dr. Butler.

I told Dr. Butler that I agreed very heartily with what he had said and described the contents of my letter to Dr. Andrews. He was somewhat reassured by what I had said. He tried to arrange a meeting with Dr. Andrews who was still not available. I left, as there was nothing more I could do before a meeting with Dr. Andrews and Dr. Butler. I intimated that I did not propose to come to the hospital again without a fresh invitation.

A few days later Dr. Andrew telephoned me to apologize for not having been present on the previous occasion. He explained that my letter had gone astray and had only now reached him, and asked me to attend a meeting with him and Dr. Butler of the sort that I had suggested in the letter and discussed with Dr. Butler.

At this meeting I emphasized that it was not I who had

suggested I conduct the project; I was happy to do this, but could not hope for any chance of success unless they both wished it and were prepared to announce to the whole staff who I was, under what arrangement I was there, what it was planned I should do, and how I would go about it.

We discussed the pros and cons of a study in which I would take an action research (consultant) role. I explained that in view of my other commitments it would be possible to arrange for about six weeks of work only. They asked whether I could complete the project in that time. I said that there could be no real end to such work: the clarification or solution of any one problem led only to the next. The question was rather whether, in the time available, we could get over the inevitable initial hump of disturbance and anxiety, to go on to something which would contain a promise of positive return. I said there was a risk that we could not do so, and it was for them to decide whether to take that risk.

Dr. Butler mentioned at this stage the important position of Miss Edwards and her staff in the division. I suggested that she be asked to join us. When she did so, Dr. Andrews described the background, making the point quite clearly that my presence was at his direct instigation. We went over the ground again, and Miss Edwards, after raising several questions, said that in her view the possible gains from my work would justify the risks. She would be happy to collaborate in the study and join in a formal invitation to me.

We went on to the question of the scope and method of my work. It was agreed by all of us that it would not be possible to include in my study any formal work on the relation of the division to the hospital administration. This would be too large a task, and one that would require us to seek agreement outside the division. I should confine myself to internal processes and relationships. I suggested that it would expedite the study, and save me from having to deal with the ambiguities of semi-confidential personal communications, if I met the staff only in groups. It was agreed, therefore, that I should meet in groups the medical staff, the nursing staff in the administrative grade, sisters in charge of wards, and the professional staff of the large laboratory which formed part of the research unit. I was given to understand that the latter included physiologists, anatomists, and neuropathologists. I suggested that, after a first round of discussions with these groups, I would report back my composite picture to Dr. Andrews, Dr. Butler, and Miss Edwards, who would remain constituted as a project committee, and then take the same picture back to the staff groups again. In this way the staff might get something from my work – though this might be merely a wider picture or an outside opinion on issues raised – and I could check and elaborate my information and observation. The project would end with a meeting with the project committee, at which we could work over this picture as finally built up and elaborated by me.[1]

This was agreed; we fixed some provisional dates for the group meetings with staff, and the following statement, signed by Dr. Andrews, Dr. Butler, and Miss Edwards, was issued:

> This is to inform you that we have invited Dr. Cyril Sofer to consider with us the ways in which we conduct and combine research and treatment in this building. Dr. Sofer is a sociologist from The Tavistock Institute of Human Relations. As Dr. Sofer's work with us is confined to a short period, he will not be able to meet everyone. We have there-

[1] My understanding of the situation of the James Division was based on a very short period of contact, and rested almost entirely on one investigatory technique (group discussion). I saw the organization at a critical phase of what was clearly a many-sided evolution that could be properly understood only in its historical context. Although the information I built up appeared sufficient to provide material for discussion and advice, it could not have done full justice to a highly complex structure and situation. My assessment of this situation would not be so close as I know it to have become in the case of the other two organizations where I carried out protracted investigations over a very much longer period. The study of the research unit nevertheless illustrates the approach that forms the subject matter of this book, the ways in which I formed and shared my impressions, and the process that ensues between the social consultant and the group whose organization he is studying and trying to help.

A central lack derived from the fact that I had neither the time nor the sanction to examine the relationship of the research unit to the hospital. It was accordingly impossible to estimate to what extent the processes I observed were attributable to 'environmental, contextual' factors. It could, of course, be observed here – as indubitably in every similar case – that the existence of the external pressures was 'used' by the staff to 'explain' real or imagined deficiencies in performance. This behaviour was inevitably accentuated by the fact that the unit and the unit-division relationship were very new, and staff were especially anxious that the new arrangements should work and the programme justify itself and themselves. The use of the external reality situation as a 'defence' does not in any way negate the fact that the foundation in a relatively tradition-bound establishment of a pioneering research unit, which needed flexibility as an essential principle of its work, was bound to lead to strain, at least in the short term.

fore arranged for him to meet a small portion of our total staff, mainly those of us who have personal experience in combining their research with the clinical operation of the division.

THE START OF THE FORMAL PROJECT

Organization of the Division

As soon as this decision was taken, Dr. Butler, Miss Edwards, and I met to expand my knowledge of the operations of the division.

They emphasized the significance of the fact that the hospital was an old-established one with its own institutionalized procedures, traditions, and structure. As consultant in charge of the division, Dr. Butler was legally responsible to the hospital for the clinical care of patients. He had directly responsible to him a senior registrar and a registrar, both of whom were, like himself, on the hospital payroll. The research unit had Dr. Andrews as its own director. He and Dr. Butler worked very closely together, as Dr. Butler had to take clinical responsibility for the patients with whom Dr. Andrews and his staff worked. The nursing staff were, like Dr. Butler, hospital employees. Although they were already working closely with one or two research projects that were starting, their allegiance was to the hospital. A complicating factor was that Miss Edwards – the assistant matron in charge of the nursing services of the division, and of a staff of six administrative-grade nurses, eight ward sisters, seventeen staff nurses, and sixty-seven assistant nurses – was responsible to the central nursing administration of the hospital, i.e. to the matron and to the medical superintendent, and not to Dr. Butler. He was not formally in a position to give instructions to nursing staff, even though he took clinical responsibility for all patients in the division. In a sense, then, there were three streams of authority in the division, emanating from Dr. Andrews (research), Dr. Butler (clinical care), and Miss Edwards (nursing).

When the research unit was set up its staff augmented the normal allocation to the division. There was accordingly a much higher staff-patient ratio here than in the hospital generally.

This was especially the case on the medical staff. Three appointments or attachments of research physicians had been made to date to Dr. Andrews's staff, and there was a vacancy for a senior research physician. It had been realized that, if the hospital-appointed core of the medical staff had only clinical responsibilities and the other doctors attached to the unit only research responsibilities, this would frustrate the object of providing for a fruitful interplay between therapy and research, and make difficulties arising out of uneven responsibilities and opportunities. Accordingly, it had been arranged that every doctor in the division – whether he was formally on the research or hospital budget – would have clinical responsibility for patients in at least one ward, as well as some opportunity for research. This excepted Dr. Andrews. Each of the three research physicians attached to Dr. Andrews was in charge of a ward, Dr. Butler took charge of one ward, and his senior registrar and registrar of two each.

Apart from financing the appointments of Dr. Andrews's staff, the research-sponsoring organization had made funds available to the hospital for a nurse with full-time research duties, and for the appointment of a small number of other nurses over and above the usual nursing establishment.

The Medical Staff

My first meeting was with the medical staff. I began by repeating, for the benefit of those who had not already met me, my task and my membership of the Tavistock Institute. I explained that Dr. Andrews had invited me to look at this organization and give my views on it; that preliminary talks had been followed by a meeting that day with him, Dr. Butler, and Miss Edwards, at which they had asked me to consider with them the ways in which research and treatment were combined in the building; and that, at my suggestion, it had been agreed that I should meet the doctors, laboratory research staff, senior sisters, and ward sisters for a first round of group discussions. I would combine my impressions in a first

FIGURE 3

ORGANIZATION OF JAMES DIVISION AND RELATIONS WITH SUPERIOR BODIES

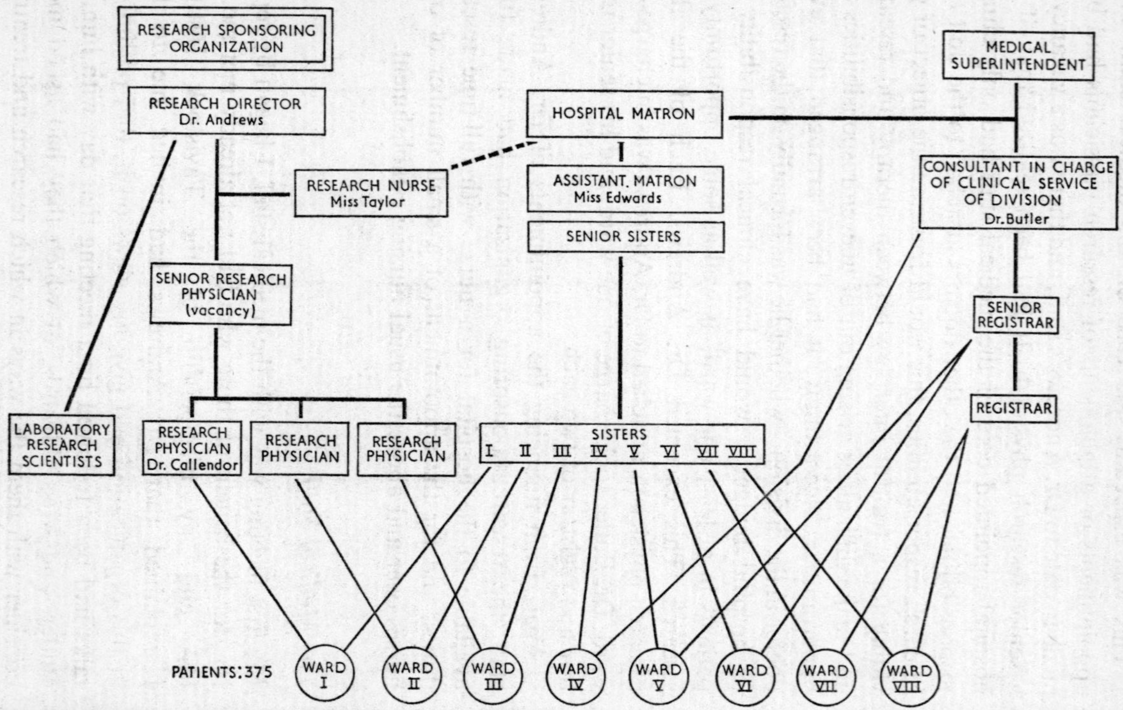

report to the project committee of Dr. Andrews, Dr. Butler, and Miss Edwards, meet the staff group again to present this picture and discuss it further, and end with a final couple of meetings with the project committee. I was working with groups because my time was short and because I wanted to concentrate on general issues rather than possibly be embarrassed by personal confidences. I emphasized that I had told the project committee that, because the work was being compressed into a very short period, little or nothing that was constructive might come of it.[1]

Members of the group said that every doctor was expected to do some research, but there was a lack of direction. Many research efforts were being made, but these were in different directions. Each doctor joining the research unit or the division's own establishment came with different ideas and expectations. While some of the doctors owed their allegiance to the hospital, others were affiliated to the research unit; the latter also differed among themselves – two held short-term appointments and one was on a training fellowship.

The group intimated that these various statuses were not clearly related to each other in a hierarchy or authority structure, though members of the research unit knew they were responsible to Dr. Andrews, and the senior registrar and the registrar knew they were responsible to Dr. Butler. Over a period of time a jockeying for position had occurred among the medical staff.

A member described how he had transferred here from another division of the hospital after difficulties had arisen about the research he had wished to initiate there. The James Division was not popular with many of the hospital physicians, since its outlook was rather outside the stream of thought to which many of the leading hospital doctors subscribed.

It was suggested that the service was suffering from growing pains. Had it been a mistake to recruit at this phase junior people rather than more experienced workers who could have prepared the way for others like themselves?

The group complained that they saw too little of the head of

[1] The same introduction was given to each other subsequent group in round one.

the research unit, and that he was too busy with administrative matters and the process of setting up the new unit to see much of their work in the wards.

They said that the policy of the division and the research unit was to allow everyone some time for research and some experience of the weight of clinical care, so as to avoid making those on the hospital payroll mere handmaidens to research. In effect, this gave a great deal of authority to the consultant in charge of the division, even over those doctors not on his staff who might consider themselves equally senior or more senior in their profession, because he was responsible to the hospital for clinical care in all the wards.

Regardless of professional seniority, each doctor had charge of one ward and had no authority outside this. Difficulties were accentuated by the fact that it had not been found possible to attract to the unit a suitable person for the post of senior clinical research worker. This would have gone a long way towards filling the gap between the research head and the rest of the medical staff attached to him.

The conflict of the principle of a research democracy with that of medical seniority had led to differing definitions of the situation between themselves. These differences were visible to the nursing staff.

It seemed to me that the consultant in charge of the division, Dr. Butler, and the most senior of the psychiatrists attached to the research unit, Dr. Callendor, had been chief competitors – and sufferers – in a vacuum created by Dr. Andrews's difficulty in finding sufficient time to involve himself actively enough with the medical staff, and by the delay in filling the senior research role. Dr. Butler was becoming, or had become, the more influential by virtue of his special legal position, his greater knowledge of the hospital, and his personal abilities. At the same time, he did not have the official status on the research side corresponding to his informal position. Also, he lacked the international scientific reputation of Dr. Andrews, and the rest of the medical staff were not altogether prepared to accept him as, in effect, deputy head of the total organization.

None of those present were senior research men. Several were fitted, by virtue of their previous training and experience, to be only research apprentices. They did not have the opportunity to work with a master. In the circumstances, I felt that there must be a pronounced gap between the high expectations placed on the unit and its probable achievements, and that all those present would suffer from being the object of hopes that they felt they would disappoint.

Laboratory Research Scientists

My next meeting was with the laboratory research workers. This meeting opened slowly, possibly because I had met none of them beforehand.

There were many questions about my role. They wanted to know how I could do my job without understanding the technicalities of pathology, anatomy, or neuropsychiatry, whether I was an efficiency expert, and whether I wished to concentrate on problems and grudges.

After some attempts at clarification, the group began to debate, with little intervention from me, whether there were any difficulties or limitations to their research that could not be solved by more time and money. One member pointed to a constraint imposed on the work by legal factors – one could not experiment physically with a patient without the explicit consent of a responsible relative. His colleagues pointed out that financial and legal constraints could be used as alibis for the research worker who lacked drive or doubted his own abilities.

A member of the group said that in the design of research they had to take into account both the constraints of the type described and the strain placed on the hospital by the recent influx of research workers. He felt that he himself had not done too badly by making certain compromises on his requirements for a study in regard to the size of his sample (which was drawn from the hospital as a whole) and the amount of preparatory clinical description of each patient in it, especially of those transferred from other divisions. He had been able to make a satisfactory, if small-scale, beginning, and had managed to enlist the interest and collaboration of both medical and nursing staff within and outside the division.

Others took up the question of lack of adequate preparatory

work on hospital patients. This was a handicap when it came to subsequent research. They would also receive greater benefit from being sited in the hospital if there were more experienced doctors in the James service.

Several felt a pressure because the people in charge had to justify the large investment in the research unit. One member thought it would be more correct to regard the pressure as internal to the individual. The group said that they were the objects of envy of people in other services of the hospital, outside this unit, and had been criticized for doing some work which was not on patients and (it was said) was irrelevant to the needs of the hospital.

They had good contacts with the nurses, not only in the course of research but also through lectures to them.

Ward Sisters

The nurses who headed the various wards showed at meetings a great deal of enthusiasm for what was going on in their wards. They said a new interest had been given them by the atmosphere of research and experimentation, and by the allocation of particular groups of patients to nurses in the course of the major clinical research project which had been begun.

The nurses said this division differed markedly from others in the hospital. The higher proportion of staff to patients made possible an improved relationship with patients. They received more information about what was going on and were co-opted more actively into the treatment team. They felt that they were contributing to changes in patients, rather than being custodians. Several had previous associations with research, but had been less actively associated with the details and had had less opportunity to contribute their own ideas.

A number of reasons had made it easy for them to collaborate with doctors in research. A research and educational tradition had existed in the James Division even before the new research unit had been established; through a natural process, nurses sympathetic to these activities had tended to stay and others to leave.

In answer to a question from me, they said they did not feel any opposition between research and clinical operations in their work. Since the research in which they were involved was on methods of treatment, the two components were indivisible. They did not consider it made any difference to them whether the doctor in charge of a ward was on the hospital payroll or attached to the research unit.

This enthusiasm was accompanied by highly critical attitudes towards the rest of the hospital. While the nurses felt they had high prestige because of their membership of this division, they felt that the hospital was too rigid in applying to their work the rules applicable to other parts of the hospital. Where, for instance, they wanted to give a patient greater freedom for the sake of an experiment, the hospital refused this.

I reminded the group that over a period of years the hospital (and the legal system of the country) had evolved practices to safeguard the interests of patients, relatives, and the general public. These could not be expected to change rapidly. Changes that might be justified for one ward or service of the hospital might not be justified for others, and therefore it might not be possible to initiate them at all.

I tried to indicate that enthusiasm for change on their part could be expected to go together with a degree of scepticism in others elsewhere in the hospital. They would have to exercise a considerable amount of self-discipline in their relations with colleagues outside the division.

If they wanted those in wider authority to change the total structure, they would need first to create confidence in themselves by showing what they could do with the present structure. In the interests of the long-term changes they wanted, they should show a readiness to compromise. One thing they could do in the meantime, with the problem cases of which they complained, was to document these, so that the effects on patients of specific administrative decisions could be traced out.

Nursing Administration

The meeting with the senior sisters (nurses in the administrative grade, including Miss Edwards) covered a more limited amount of ground more intensively. There was some discussion of the problem of allocating nurses to participate in research projects, and also of how nurses could be helped to cope with the needs of patients outside research groups when the needs of the two types of patient were in conflict.

There was present in the group, as a person of equal status with the administrators, Miss Taylor, a nurse who had been specifically designated the division's 'research nurse'. Much interest centred around her role and I concentrated on this. Miss Taylor said that as the division's research nurse she was responsible to the hospital matron and to Dr. Andrews rather than to Miss Edwards. She did some teaching of student nurses who passed through the service. She spent most of her time, however, helping with the administration of the main current clinical research project, seeing that the nurses carried out the required recording, collecting the schedules they filled in, advising them on the research part of their work, and seeing that the patient groups were kept together in the way required by the research design. At the same time, she was studying the attitudes of the nursing staff towards their work, and advising the matron on the implications for the hospital as a whole of new nursing practices developed in the division.

I suggested that her operations must bristle with problems. I was sure that she could not carry out her duties without the close collaboration of Miss Edwards and without discussing with her the work of the nurses with whom she came into contact. Miss Edwards could at any time make her work impossible, for instance, by indicating to a nurse that she had heard from the research nurse something to her detriment. At this stage Miss Edwards responded, 'At any time I can pull the rug out from under Miss Taylor.'

I underlined the point that as supervisor of research Miss Taylor was the recipient of information and confidences which nurses would not wish her to communicate elsewhere, yet, as a recognized senior nurse of the hospital, she was obliged to help in the administration. Furthermore, she placed herself in an awkward position by regarding herself as an independent research worker on nursing attitudes and performance. When a nurse discussed work with her, she would wonder how this was regarded – as a request for advice, as an item of research data, or as something that would be passed on to her line supervisors. The content of her work on the research side seemed most uneven – she must be part independent research worker, part clerical assistant to the doctors undertaking the research project, part consultant, and part disciplinarian.

As I made these remarks, Miss Taylor and her colleagues responded with extreme interest in the subject. Many concrete incidents were quoted to illustrate that these problems were far from hypothetical. Some of the difficulties in her role were those that it had been attempted to avoid on the physicians' side by spreading the research component of the work.

I said that while this role was clearly a very difficult one to work – or to work with – I could see how it could have several positive effects. It was an advantage to have someone in the division to feed the practical implications of experimental work into the wider hospital programme, and to smooth the way for research. I suggested that we return to the subject of the research nurse's role once the second round of group discussions was under way – I would be happy to contribute suggestions at that stage if I had any.

REPORTING EARLY FINDINGS TO PROJECT COMMITTEE

The first round of discussions having been completed, I was ready now to report back to the project committee. I made the points set out below and we then returned to them one by one for detailed discussion.

I said that, as I saw it, the extent to which the division could experiment in patient care was limited by rules and practices relating to the hospital as a whole. To secure greater flexibility for their special needs, members of the division would have to display a preparedness to adapt research and experimental designs to an extent consistent with the legal and professional obligations of the hospital. They would have to manifest their appreciation of the forces that make a hospital administration cautious in innovation, and try to earn the right to greater permissibility through this and through the quality of the work done. If the total context was assumed as the given environment for their work, this might reduce the diversion of energy from internal tasks to problems posed by the nature of that environment.

It would be helpful if the division could become officially recognized as the 'research and development' arm of the hospital and, as such, be empowered to experiment in certain approved ways on behalf of the total organization, and to test certain possibilities over a small number of cases on its behalf. If a policy of this type was adopted, the relationship of these experiments to the rest of the hospital might be studied by a social research worker interested in organization change. He could collaborate further with the heads of the hospital in considering the practical implications for the hospital of past and current social research on mental hospitals.

While the conduct of research had had an excellent effect on nursing morale, this could lead to depreciation of past tradition and over-evaluation of investigation and change for their own sake.

Some type of group procedure might be considered in the allocation of nursing staff to the various combinations of research and treatment which now constituted the nurses' tasks. A group of nurses might be given topics or problems to discuss, and at least two observers could watch characteristic forms of behaviour in the group situation and try to judge, on the basis of this and other experience with the persons concerned, who was likely to do best in what type of real-life situation. Past experience with procedures of this type suggested that they reduced to some extent the margin of error inevitable in placement.

The position of research nurse appeared to contain current or potential incompatibilities. The content of her job, as now emerging, varied greatly in technical level. It was not clear to what extent the person in this post should be a research assistant or an independent research worker. It would be difficult, if not impossible, for anyone in this position to combine superintendence of the research duties of nurses with studies or consultations with the same nurses. The first role would debar her from receiving communications required for the second. It would be very easy for her responsibilities towards those nurses whose research duties she supervised or whom she studied to become inconsistent with her responsibilities towards the division's assistant matron and towards the overall hospital nursing administration. There seemed to be some inconsistency between concentrating responsibility for research in one nurse and spreading a similar responsibility widely among medical staff.

I suggested that it might be desirable to make a detailed study of nurses' roles as they were now developing in the division. This might cover the main specific duties expected to be completed by the nurse or actually carried out by her, the relationships involved, the obligations and rights and opportunities of the nurse, and the demands and satisfactions of the job. A description of this type could provide opportunities for working through to a clarification of what was psychologically and sociologically involved in nursing and in participating in psychiatric experiments, and might assist in selection, placement, and training.

Concluding, I said that a vacuum had appeared in the sphere of the doctors because of the difficulty of recruiting experienced clinicians and clinical research workers, and the lack of opportunities for supervised research apprenticeship. Under existing conditions the research achievements that could realistically be expected on the clinical side must be more modest than the investment would seem to imply.

Reactions of the Committee

Committee members were quick to accept my suggestion that too much was being projected onto the hospital and that this was serving to divert attention from their own internal problems. We discussed the possibility of a prolonged action-research project being conducted with the hospital, which would include attention to their own unit as a research and development arm and perhaps feed in some current sociological findings and approaches – though I felt that I had to take care to emphasize that I would not be able to undertake this.

They agreed that group procedures for the allocation of

nursing staff might be helpful. The selection would be improved, and so would subsequent collaboration, if senior medical staff were co-opted into such procedures. But this very novel innovation might be felt to infringe the rights of the nursing administration and also to raise the question of the reciprocal rights of nurses to make a formal contribution towards the allocation of doctors – an even more revolutionary idea.

The committee seemed pleased to have attention drawn to anomalies in the role of research nurse and to the potential difficulties, though it was not yet evident whether anything could be done about them. They pointed out that her administrative duties in the current research project had an important positive side in bringing her into close daily contact with ward work.

When we reached the topic of relations among the medical staff, Dr. Andrews emphasized the extent to which administrative demands kept him from contact with the staff. He was appalled at the amount of his time taken up in trying to provide conditions for effective work rather than in settling down to a research job. This part of the discussion was to some extent affected by our beginning theme about the projection of difficulties onto hospital administration. Little could be done to recruit psychiatrists with good research experience. The unit was tied to salary scales that made it impossible to compete with purely clinical appointments which also offered some opportunity for private practice. I suggested that consideration be given to the establishment of special research fellowships, carrying salaries equal to the clinical scale together with special opportunities for research and advanced training. Dr. Butler said one negative consequence of this was that doctors elsewhere in the hospital would feel discriminated against: they were already envious of special facilities in the James Division and felt that they were disparaged as people of inferior status. I said I saw no reason why they should not be eligible for fellowships – in any case one cannot refrain from administrative steps necessary for the achievement of a task because some unsuccessful candidates for posts would be hurt at being passed over.

SECOND ROUND OF STAFF MEETINGS

Having made my first report to the project committee, I went on to the second round of staff meetings. I was now in a position to give something back to them in the form of the composite picture I had built up and the issues which seemed to me to be important. I could in some cases make suggestions or comments on actual problems.

Nursing Administration

I began the second meeting with the senior sisters by reporting the main points I had made to the project committee.

I made certain suggestions for restructuring the position of research nurse. Line responsibility for the research duties of nurses should be moved from Miss Taylor to Miss Edwards and her executive chain. This would return operational supervision to its proper place, help to make research a part of the nurses' job rather than an imposition or extra burden, prevent a possible playing off of Miss Taylor against line heads, and free her to act as consultant to nursing staff. She should help to train nurses for their participation in research projects, act as consultant on nursing aspects of research, and watch the implications of research experiments for hospital nursing and nurse-training practices.

She should not undertake formal studies of nurses' attitudes, but take account of the possible effect of nursing behaviour on the patients during experiments, so that the results of this could be evaluated and assessed. Any observations, comments, interpretations, should be made only in the interest of projects. If she wished to undertake research on nurses' attitudes as such, this should be done elsewhere than in her own division, because it suggested non-reciprocity in her relationships with the staff and would damage her role as consultant-adviser to the nurses.

I went over again the procedures they might adopt in nurse placement, based on group tasks modelled on real problems. This might help to reduce error, objectify selections in a public way, and indicate that the crucial basis of staff selection and allocation was the type of relationship formed by different people in different situations. Miss Edwards was by now very favourable to the idea and was interested in using group methods for her next placements.

The Medical Staff

Both Dr. Andrews and Dr. Butler were present at my meeting with the physicians.

I went over the main points as made to the project committee, and repeated the suggestions I had made to the senior sisters so that the implications of these could be discussed here if necessary.

I emphasized that by 'explaining' their difficulties in terms of outside barriers they would reify these. People outside would catch on to their attitude and be tempted to act in the way they suggested. An undesirable type of unwitting collusion might develop. They should take the hospital environment as given and show what they could do in present circumstances. In this way they might earn the right to greater flexibility.

The medical staff had difficulty in comprehending my remarks regarding new procedures for the selection or allocation of nurses. They interpreted me as recommending that they participate as selectors. I suggested they accept the fact that Miss Edwards was responsible for such selection, but indicate to her the types of relationship they would wish the nurses to be able to form in each case. Possibly the selection committee could be Miss Edwards, an assistant, and two advisers – the research nurse and the doctor concerned.

A member asked if the assistant matron in a division like theirs should be a research trained person. I gave my opinion that it would be most productive to work from the existing position.

On the subject of their internal relationships, I told them my conclusion that part of the trouble was that, in the vacuum left by the lack of someone to guide research apprentices, many people lacked confidence in their ability to do their job well. A person in that position would inevitably attack colleagues in an unwitting effort to hinder them in their own work, so others would be failures too. One should avoid going into collusion in such circumstances by attacking back, but should redirect the person and oneself to the task. Dr. Andrews supported this heartily.

I was asked if I thought difficulties sprang from the existence of two systems of authority – the research and the clinical. Did I not think there was a need for greater role clarity? I replied that in their present situation a great deal of ambiguity and spontaneous adjustment and role creation was inevitable. I said emphasis on structural terms and issues had the effect of taking attention off the need for individuals to find bases for co-operation among themselves.

Dr. Andrews elaborated an idea that the unit might participate in an integrated city-wide training programme. This could provide a wider set of career possibilities for people who could start in one segment of this teaching-practice system and move to others.

We discussed the need for the medical staff to have joint tasks. One joint task could be an attempt to show the hospital what they could do in present circumstances.

It was agreed that the programme of the unit should provide for some posts in which people could attempt research projects manageable in a short-term appointment of a year or two.

In making it clear that I would not be meeting this group again, I repeated that I would be reporting back to the project committee again. I hoped the committee would return to them with any news or action points.

Laboratory Research Staff

At my second meeting with the laboratory staff I gave a similar review of the main emerging points. There was a first comment of agreement about the wisdom of accepting the present total organization as given.

The question arose again of the need for a wider range of clinical contact. They saw too few acute cases. They needed to see patients at different stages of illness rather than only patients whose illness had been stabilized. They wanted an easier, more spontaneous relationship with the admission division, with which they could co-operate, as a rule, only with formal sanction. They felt they needed more opportunities for 'experiments of opportunity' which could best arise from informal interaction with colleagues. Though formal occasions for seeing intake case presentations were open to them, these had not become institutionalized.

I was not clear about the extent to which they actually availed themselves of existing opportunities and how much these complaints were defensive.

There was some discussion about the possibility of an overall social research project on the hospital. One man suggested that inquiry into causes of conflict would create the conflict. I suggested the alternative possibility that such a project might bring social relationships and stresses into the realm of matters accepted as natural processes, and therefore susceptible to investigation and action.

We discussed ways of developing clinical and laboratory research, and referred to the need for short projects which junior people could conduct in what would virtually amount to a short research apprenticeship; the possibilities for longer-term contracts for others if the idea of a city-wide training scheme came into force; and the attraction sabbatical years here, with no duties, might have for senior people.

Someone pointed out that there was a criticism of the hospital implicit in the establishment of the research unit (i.e. it implied that the hospital was not doing enough research before). The group felt that other people in the hospital, especially those who had previously been doing research, envied them their special research opportunities. As a result, they said they felt a pressure to justify themselves.

Ward Sisters

At my second meeting with the ward sisters I ran through the points I had made to the project committee at the midway meetings.

Some discussion followed on the projection I had pointed out, and also on the amount of 'splitting' facilitated by the division of labour practised by hospitals. As could be expected, this was apparent in their own situation – the division of labour made it easy to blame someone else whenever there was a chance of something failing.

The group informed me that, following my suggestions, the duties of research nurse had now changed. They had noticed the difficulties after the potential for trouble had been pointed out to them.

In regard to collaboration within the division, there was some discussion of the publicly unrecognized role of nurses in teaching new doctors aspects of their work, and of the extent to which nurses could sabotage an unpopular doctor.

Compliments were paid about the way I had carried out my work and the use it had had for them. I thought these overdone and pointed out that this over-admiration could provide a rationale for not carrying on with the work I had started or the 'improvements' set in motion. Since, as they knew, I was just about to leave, they could 'regress' if they wished and take the line that as I was no longer there it was no use trying to improve things.

FINAL REPORTS TO PROJECT COMMITTEE

I returned now to the project committee for two final meetings.

I reminded the group of our previous discussion of the fact that the situation of the James division within the hospital lent itself to the projection of difficulties onto the external hospital administration, and to a possible 'reification' of negative attitudes towards those in the division.

My further consideration had led me to the conclusion that the division was likely to be handicapped by its adoption of the traditional hospital pattern of internal administration, as this pattern characteristically divided responsibility in a way that reduced accountability for whole tasks. Under the present system, there was ample opportunity in the division for any staff member to avoid the personal conflict inevitably involved in full responsibility for his particular area of work by pointing to the opposition of other people with competing responsibilities.

It might be possible to redress this situation somewhat by arranging responsibilities in such a way that each individual could experience and resolve the conflicts appropriate to his role – e.g. in regard to clinical risks to be taken with a patient in the interests of research – rather than by dividing conflicting responsibilities among people in such a way that they could blame each other for being over-conservative or too venturesome.

I asked whether an example could not be set to the whole unit if Dr. Andrews became clinical as well as research head. This met with an unpopular reception. Dr. Andrews said it would make his research duties impossible, and Dr. Butler suggested that I did not appreciate the weight of administrative work that went with his post.

I suggested that a fundamental contribution might be made by the fuller integration of the division at senior level, e.g. Dr. Andrews, Dr. Butler, and Miss Edwards might meet regularly and frequently to brief each other on recent events in their respective spheres and discuss their main intentions before finalizing them. If it was to be effective, such a procedure should be formally announced and firmly institutionalized within the division.

In regard to the matter of group selection of nurses, I reported that the senior doctors had suggested they might participate in such procedures. I said that this did not seem to me to be unreasonable, provided that it was understood that the final responsibility for choice was that of the assistant matron, and provided also that she received opportunities to express her views on the selection of other staff, including doctors. The committee seemed intrigued at these novel possibilities, and agreed that if the medical staff wanted the rights they had requested this must be reciprocal.

On the whole the committee seemed to agree on the need for more joint responsibility for major decisions within the division.

I reported that I had suggested that the component of research administration in the role of research nurse be handed to the sister in charge of each ward, and that the nurses planned to implement this. The intention would be to reduce potential 'splitting' in this area, to make participation in research a taken-for-granted part of nursing in the division, and to free the research nurse for activities of a more consultative character. The committee seemed pleased with this suggestion and the way it might work out.

I said that a difference persisted between the expectations of the medical staff regarding the extent to which Dr. Andrews would be involved in their research, and the extent to which he could in fact be involved. It should be made clear to them that for some time ahead his practical involvement in their work would be minimal. This would make it easier to operate on a reality-oriented basis, and remove both a potential grievance and a potential rationalization for possible limitations in achievement. Dr. Andrews replied that he expected to be able to set aside more time to work with the doctors in the near future.

A need existed for a research programme that would allow for projects of widely differing duration. This would take into account the differences in the needs of various types of staff who might be attracted to the division. Such a programme could be described in a brochure and receive wide distribution. The programme should be viewed as an important public relations venture. The planning of such a publication could become a task of a representative group formed from the whole division, and the completion of specific sections could be delegated to several people. This could give a realistic flavour to specific sections, and underline for members of the division the fact that they were involved in a collective enterprise.

As requested by the laboratory group, I reported their need for more contact with a sample of such acute cases as entered the hospital, and for research into the change from acute to chronic stages in illness. The project committee said that a possible step in this direction might be the manning by the unit of one ward in the admission division of the hospital. I suggested that an alternative or additional step might be the involvement of members of the present admission division in a collaborative research project with the James Division – for instance, one on the transition from acute to chronic mental illness. This might help to bridge the gap between the division and the rest of the hospital, as well as provide the needed access to a wider variety of clinical material.

One more meeting took place, about a week later. The object of this last meeting was to take up any additional points that might have occurred to any of us in the meanwhile, and to review the way in which the project had gone.

By this time the group had in their hands a note I had completed on the previous meeting, to fulfil a request from Dr. Andrews for some record of the work and of the most important points made in discussion. We went through the main points again.

Dr. Andrews asked whether I thought the meetings that I had suggested should take place regularly between themselves should be extended to include representatives of the hospital administration. I gave my opinion that in this respect at least the solidarity of the division should receive priority over the need to constitute an open system with the hospital.

He and his colleagues said they had found my suggestion regarding the research nurse's role helpful, and were acting on this. As it had been structured it had worked for a while but it was now clear that it was unlikely to continue doing so. I took the opportunity to say that theoretically unworkable arrangements could often be sustained by the goodwill and determination of the people concerned. This obviously had wider reference than the role under discussion.

Dr. Andrews repeated his intention to participate more with the medical staff. He said that leaving them alone had its positive side, as the cream tended to rise naturally. I commented that, while there were certain advantages in a process of natural selection, young people needed help in initiating research, more especially in seeing the relation of an 'interesting' clinical event to a research problem; they also needed guidance in applying the research skills they had been taught to problems they would like to solve, and help in the formulation of 'researchable' questions – in short, a research apprenticeship.

We discussed briefly the way this short project had gone. Most of the remarks were complimentary to me, though Dr. Andrews said that I had not shown proper appreciation of the place of laboratory research. He was surprised to hear in my reply that I had not yet been shown this side of the work, and offered to remedy this immediately our meeting ended.

There was some discussion of resistance and co-operation in work of this type. It was suggested that I had encountered little or no hostility to my work in this project. I intimated rather that negative feelings invariably arise in such work and that I had found no more and no less of such feelings than usual.

The group emphasized that they found it valuable to test their views and feelings with someone who had a different vantage point. It was agreed that where such help was attempted the person concerned should not be responsible to someone within the organization. I suggested that he should have an independent technical base with colleagues whom he could consult.

The group asked me whether I might be prepared to continue such work with them, or conduct a project with the larger hospital administration of the type I had adumbrated and illustrated. I repeated this would not be possible.

We discussed the possibility of finding an alternative social scientist in the locality.

A member of the group said that if a new person were found he would probably be someone who would have to learn how to work as I had done. The hospital would have to be tolerant of him. I mentioned that one function of over-rating me and the work I had done would be to provide a rationale for letting these matters drop now that I was going, or for being less co-operative with anyone who followed. The meeting – and the project – ended at this point.

CHAPTER 3

AN EDUCATIONAL SETTING

The Helmsley Department of Management and Production Engineering

PRELIMINARIES

TOWARDS the end of 1953, before I was a member of the Tavistock Institute, I became acquainted with Mr. David Richardson at a seminar held at the Institute. Mr. Richardson was the newly appointed head of the Department of Management and Production Engineering at the Helmsley Technical College.[1] We both had an interest in the work done at the Tavistock Institute and had both known the then chairman of the management committee, Dr. A. T. M. Wilson, for some years. There was a further link between Helmsley and the Institute, in that an influential member of the governing body[2] of the college was managing director of a company which had been closely associated with the Institute over many years.

The position of Mr. Richardson's department in its college and County Council setting was as shown in *Figure 4*.

Mr. Richardson told me that he was planning a research project in connection with the work of his department, and

[1] Helmsley Technical College was one of several technical colleges administered and maintained by the Medburn County Council, which is a local education authority and, as such, is required to secure the provision for its area of adequate facilities for 'further education'. The college was organized into six departments, each of which had its own head. Academic grades of work ranged from teaching for apprentices to teaching for university higher degrees.

[2] The governing body consisted of part-time members, appointed by the County Council, to 'have the general supervision of the college, carry out schemes of instruction approved by the County Council, and submit annual estimates'. A college principal was responsible for the internal organization, management, and discipline of all departments of the college.

had submitted an application for a research grant to the U.K. Department of Scientific and Industrial Research under the Conditional Aid Programme. The objectives of the research were to examine the function and possibilities of a technical college department of management and production engineering in servicing industry; to examine, with the department, its services and structure; and to help members of the department to establish the most effective feedback mechanism between industry and themselves.

He asked whether I would be interested to lead the research team that would carry out this work. Our conversations led to an understanding that I would probably do so on my return from a five-month trip to the United States, to which I was already committed, if the research application was successful and if suitable administrative arrangements could be made for the project. This was a problem from the beginning. The original plan had been for the full-time employment of a research team at the college, paid out of the research grant, which would be administered by the County Council. With discussion, the realization grew that such a research team – having as its purpose the study of the department's structure and services – could not easily form part of the department. Nor could the head of the department suitably belong, even part time, to a research team obliged to bring an external objectivity to the work done by him and his staff. Some form of separate unit seemed more appropriate.

Our preliminary discussions had left this question unresolved by the time I departed for America. It continued to be discussed by all parties concerned – Mr. Richardson, the principal of his college, the Board of governors, officers and committee members of the County Council, and the two or three research workers other than myself who had similarly been approached to join the research team.

While everyone could see that a research unit separate from the management department would be essential for the task, if a frank assessment of its operations was to be made, on what basis was the research team to be employed and to whom would it be responsible? The prospective research workers wanted to be sure that they could take up whatever topics

FIGURE 4

RELATIONSHIP OF MANAGEMENT DEPARTMENT TO THE COLLEGE AND COUNTY COUNCIL

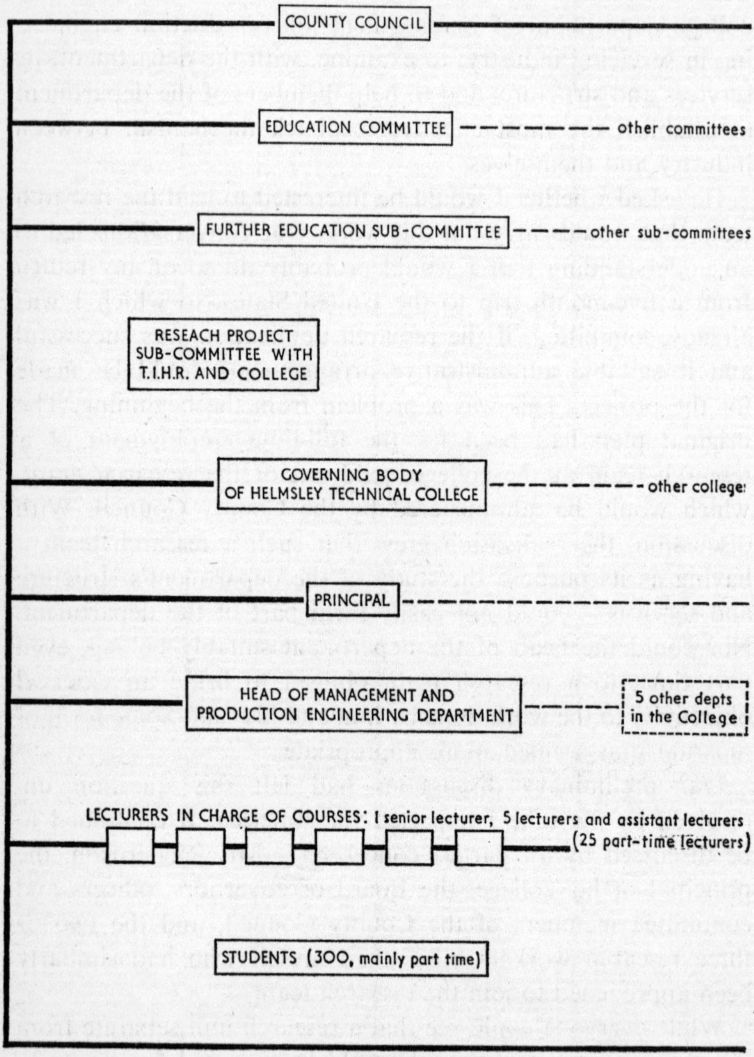

within their terms of reference they and the departmental staff chose to study. They foresaw that this might sometimes include the relation of members of the department to the college principal and the County Council. The County Council, on the other hand, needed security against undue disturbance of on-going work in the department, against possible by-passing of channels, and against unsanctioned or irresponsible publicity being given to research findings. Since the County Council is an elected body organized on party lines there is always a section of the press interested to secure ammunition against the party currently in power. Having no precedent for the employment of full-time research workers examining the work of a technical college department, the County Council officials sought arrangements for engaging the research team essentially similar, with respect to administrative control, to those for engaging teaching or clerical staff. If the research team were on the college staff, what they did could be watched and controlled. This was naturally unacceptable to the prospective research workers as being unduly restrictive to research.

Meantime, the study was delayed. The grant-providing body, the Department of Scientific and Industrial Research, was unable to pay out any of the funds, which it had by now agreed in principle to make available, until satisfactory arrangements had been made for the conduct of the research. Two or three of the prospective research workers found themselves without employment while they waited for arrangements to be completed.

At some stages feelings ran high. Although the majority of the people concerned now wanted a research project conducted, and the necessary money and people were available, everyone was being frustrated by a mutual inability to agree upon appropriate arrangements.

After several months of discussion Dr. Wilson, as head of the Tavistock Institute, and a member of the D.S.I.R. committee that decided research grants in this area, was asked to help to get the project started. An informal meeting was called between himself, the chairman of the County Council, and the chairman of the responsible education committee. Dr. Wilson suggested that the research workers should be provided with an independent base outside the college from which they could work with a reasonable degree of objectivity and freedom, but should guarantee professional confidentiality in respect of research data until approval was given to their publication outside the situation where they had been collected.

These suggestions met with the approval of all parties. Discussion ensued on the best technical base for the work. It was agreed to ask a university or research organization to provide a base. It was, however, thought unlikely that a university department would be willing to enter into an agreement which would limit rights to publication of research.

Eventually, by common consent, the wish was expressed that the Institute would itself undertake to employ a research team and conduct the research on the suggested pattern. This would not be administratively difficult as the arrangements were not unlike those customarily made by the Institute when entering into research or advisory relationships. The County Council made a formal request to the Institute to appoint a research team and accept responsibility for the project, and the Institute agreed to do so.

A liaison committee was formed between the County Council, the college, and the Tavistock Institute. It was to meet half-yearly. Its objects would be to further the aims of the research and provide a formal opportunity for any of the parties represented to intimate at any time that they wished the research to proceed no further. This included the Institute, which could cease the research if at any time it was decided that the conditions under which the research team was being permitted to work were unsatisfactory.

On the assurances of the County Council, the college, and the Institute, that arrangements had now been made to provide a base for the research team and for access to the college, the grant-providing body agreed to start paying the money to the Institute, and the Institute appointed a research team. Dr. Wilson himself was to act as principal investigator and to devote one-sixth of his time to oversight of the project, I was appointed to take executive responsibility for the research, and Mr. G. J. Hutton, formerly of the Tavistock Clinic, was to be the third member. Two-thirds of my time and the whole of Mr. Hutton's time were to be devoted to the research. Other staff members at the Institute would join in the project as and when the need for their help arose.

THE START OF THE FORMAL STUDY

The study started on 1 June 1954.[1] Mr. Hutton and I began by preparing a draft operational plan describing the objectives of the research, the groups whose collaboration would be sought, and the ways in which we would try to do our work.

It was clearly understood by all parties that the research would involve members of the department in close collaboration with us, and that we would not only collect information relevant to the objectives of the research, but help the department (and, where necessary, the college and the County Council) in the consideration of the practical implications of our observations. This component of the work was explicitly written into the operational plan.

We showed the draft operational plan to the County Council officer responsible for further education, who agreed that work could begin with the college, and then to the college principal, who agreed that the research team could begin with the management department.

As the initiator of the project and the person most identified with it, Mr. Richardson, the head of the management department, was eager that we should learn about the work and problems of his department as quickly as possible, and help him and his colleagues in the consideration of practice and policy. While he was anxious to protect his own role from encroachment, he was keenly interested in making arrangements which would enable us to work effectively, and hopeful that his staff would understand our role, help us, and accept help from us.

We discussed our research plan in detail with his full-time colleagues, together and individually, and also with the much larger part-time staff. Apart from Mr. Richardson, the full-time teaching staff consisted at that time of Mr. Cook (senior lecturer in production engineering), Mr. Dale (lecturer in pro-

[1] It ended on 31 May 1956.

duction engineering), Mr. Emmett (assistant lecturer in production engineering), and Mr. Gray (lecturer in management). Mr. Cook and Mr. Dale had been in the department for a period of years. Mr. Emmett and Mr. Gray were new to the department and had joined it largely on Mr. Richardson's initiative. Apart from being recent arrivals at the college, Mr. Richardson, Mr. Emmett, and Mr. Gray differed from Mr. Cook and Mr. Dale in that they were university graduates,[1] and in the fact that they all had previous experience in sociological or psychological research. The very much larger part-time staff were mainly employees of industrial firms who taught at the college in the evenings; like the full-time staff they were a mixture of relatively old-established (and on the whole conservative) teachers and of new choices by Mr. Richardson.

The reactions of Mr. Richardson's colleagues to us, our plans, and our methods of work, were less enthusiastic than his own and sometimes quite negative. Several of the individuals concerned had been consulted by Mr. Richardson about the project from its earliest planning stages. Most had heard something about it, but a few (especially of the large body of part-timers) knew little or nothing about it. There were many requests for information about the detailed objectives of the project, the work of the Institute, and the methods that would be employed to secure the necessary information. Most of the teachers saw that the research could provide them with information about the industrial backgrounds of their students and the practical usefulness of what they were taught. On the other hand, they were nervous about unfavourable judgements which we might make, and about the possibility that we might throw up information indicating that one or other course was of little value to students. Several staff members – including some who were on the whole favourably disposed to the work – felt that it was obscure whether we were responsible to them or to their employers, and whether they were really free not to co-operate in the research if they did not wish to do so.

These anxieties were especially acute in view of Mr. Richardson's appointment and the changes which had begun to

[1] Like many other British engineers, Mr. Cook and Mr. Dale were qualified in their field through the professional engineering institution to which they belonged, without having a university education.

come with it. He was younger than most of his colleagues, had not worked in a technical college before, had no direct industrial experience, and knew little about the engineering side of his department's work; he was a psychologist with a university research background strange to most of his colleagues, and was known to be *avant garde* in approach, even for a social scientist. We were closely identified by the staff with him, and with the social scientist who had joined him on the teaching staff, and were seen as reinforcements for his novel and threatening viewpoints.

His colleagues pointed out that the College Staff Association would wish to know exactly how the research might affect their interests and those of other departments. Partly on their initiative, the Staff Association called a meeting to discuss the research project, and asked Mr. Hutton and myself to attend. About forty people were present. We were asked searching (and often very hostile) questions about the nature, objectives, and methods of the project. Many members said they doubted whether it was desirable. They thought the management department staff were taking considerable risks in collaborating with us; they showed themselves anxious to protect their colleagues in that department against possible damage through the project, and apprehensive lest the project 'spread' at a later stage to other departments. They wanted to know how the project had originated, who had wanted it, whether reports would be made on the efficiency of individual teachers, whether we were qualified through technical training or teaching experience to study technical teaching (the implication being that we were not), whether staff members would be discussed with their superiors, what powers we possessed, and what the 'real' motivation of the research was.

On a proposal from the floor a motion was put to the meeting that the Association recommend its members in the management department not to co-operate with the research team. This was vigorously debated. Speaking against the motion, a teacher in another department said that if the management department wanted the research and was satisfied about the way it would be done, the Association should accept this situation. The research did not directly affect other departments. There had been suspicion and fear that the project constituted an attempt by the local authority to 'get at' the staff, but the necessary assurance from the research team had been given. The research might benefit members of the college by informing them on industrial needs. He was supported by a colleague who said that it would be risky in the extreme for the Tavistock Institute and the research team to behave in an unethical way towards the college staff, that the people involved had professional reputations to maintain, and that these facts were in themselves guarantees for the college.

After further discussion on both sides the motion was heavily defeated.

At a further meeting (to which we were not invited) the Staff Association resolved that it noted with interest that a research project was to be initiated in the department of management, and would welcome the opportunity to study the full results and implications of this research as it proceeded.

By this time Mr. Hutton and I had worked over the operational plan with members of the department and made some alterations of detail. We submitted the plan to the college governing body for their information and advice. We attended a meeting of this body and described how the plan had been prepared in collaboration with the management department on the basis of our original draft. At the same meeting the arrangements which had been made for the continued sanctioning of the project by the research project committee were described by a County Council official in attendance.

The general blessing and interest of the governors soon became clear. Members had already become acquainted with the proposal for a research project during the negotiations earlier described. They had voiced many of the same reservations and doubts as County Council representatives. But now they were prepared to support the research, as they were satisfied on the issue of professional responsibility, and suitable arrangements had been made with the County Council.

The governing body formally approved our operational plan, stated that so far as they were concerned the research could proceed, and asked to see interim research reports.

In the course of obtaining the formal consent of each body

or individual, we learned a great deal about the workings of the department and of the organization around it, and about the loci of power and influence. We saw the whole structure at work upon a task – the task of getting the research under way.

Equally important was the fact that during these negotiations and discussions the people concerned were getting to know us and getting to know each other better. We were all exploring each other's attitudes and outlook, testing each other's co-operativeness, and learning the rights and obligations attached to each other's roles so far as the research was concerned. The department, college, and County Council were testing our integrity and trying to make quite certain that we were unlikely to behave irresponsibly – a *modus vivendi* was being sought.

We had deliberately tried throughout this opening phase of the research to build up a professional role whose nature and limits would be clearly understood, and to demonstrate in these preliminary negotiations and explorations how we would behave when the substantive part of the research got under way.

We had sought occasions on which the co-operating groups – and especially the members of the management department with whom relations would be closest – could voice any doubts and anxieties about the research and its possible consequences. Field studies of this type characteristically arouse anxiety, as they make people uneasy about whether they are performing their tasks adequately, about the motives and trustworthiness of the research worker, and about the possibility that a precedent of 'rights to investigate' will be established. We felt that it was best to try to deal with these difficulties as and when they arose, rather than attempt to deny them, or cope later on, near the stages of attempted implementation or publication, with their consequences.

We were soon busy collecting information about courses, classes, students, staff, relationships with firms, and so on – which staff members helped us to gather. In some cases we asked the staff individually or in a group for particular information, or staff referred us to department records. At our request, staff advised us on what firms should be contacted and what points of special interest should be followed up there. They helped in the design of a questionnaire to be completed by students. They helped us to understand the functions of the various professional institutions interested in the teaching of management studies and production engineering.

Individual members of the department began to seek advice from us, especially on the content and structure of new courses. The realization grew that we could be used for help and support, especially for advice on teaching of the social sciences. There were some signs of dependence on us, and the related wish to receive the whole of our attention; this was evidenced through questions about what we did when not at the college, through irritation that we had not been available when something important had happened, or through requests for reports on progress.

It was helpful to teachers in the department to explain their work and discuss problems in its execution, quite apart from the advice which they received.

Frequent discussions were by now taking place. We arranged to meet members of the department at least once a week to receive information from them; to feed back to them our impressions and emerging findings as our own knowledge and understanding grew; to take up their responses to what we reported; and to discuss any practical implications of new data, or new definitions of the situation. In addition there were numerous conversations and consultations with individual teachers, and especially between Mr. Richardson, as head of the department, and myself. He and I remained in close touch throughout the project.

We arranged a procedure with the department for the circulation to wider groups of the research material – including that on their own behaviour – we were collecting. Any document we had prepared would be presented first to a meeting of full-time staff, then to the college principal, and then to the County Council. Any of these groups or individuals could attempt to correct what we had said if he thought the comment inaccurate or unjust, or could refuse to let the document go through to the next stage.

SOME EARLY FINDINGS

The Student Population

At the time of the study, the department dealt with about three hundred students each year, most of them male junior industrial employees with industrial or commercial experience, who attended evening classes. Half of these were working towards qualifications in management studies awarded by the British Institute of Management and Ministry of Education. A third were working towards qualifications in production engineering leading towards associate membership of the Institution of Production Engineers. In both cases students attended these classes mainly on their own initiative and paid their own fees. The remainder of the students, which included most of the full-time ones, were taking college-designed courses on work study techniques and management studies. These students were nearly all nominated by their employers, who send them to college and pay the college fees.

We found that students took a great deal of trouble to get to the college. Many travelled considerable distances after a full day's work and were often unable to secure a meal before their classes. The physical conditions under which they studied were poor; the building was noisy, and they often sat at children's desks, because the premises served as a school during the day.

Students for the management and production engineering certificate (i.e. the great majority) were taking this trouble in the hope that the courses or the formal qualifications would contribute to their career aim. Their ambitions were quite modest; they regarded the top posts in industry as more or less reserved for university graduates or those of higher social class. Because they wanted training which was related to their careers rather than of general educational value, they showed a decided preference in their classes for the more obviously and immediately relevant subjects.

In intellectual capacity (as we found with intelligence tests given to a volunteer sample) the students were roughly equivalent to a university undergraduate population or to the general run of applicants for management traineeships in industry.

While the main criteria for admission to classes were prior educational standard and intellectual capacity to follow the course, we found that many students in fact lacked the personal qualifications for promotion to management. They were pinning too much hope on courses and qualifications in management studies. They were more dependent and less certain of themselves than one would expect potential managers to be. They had inaccurate conceptions of themselves to match against the positions they wanted to take up in industry. The personal problems in this area were drawn dramatically to our attention when we carried out a promise we had made to report back, to those individuals who wished this, the scores they had achieved in the intelligence tests, and to discuss with them the meaning of the results. The most delicate and painful interviews were with the substantial proportion of young men of high intelligence, who were nevertheless failing to achieve their ambitions.

Although registered for courses, many of the students retained deep doubts about what academic training could do for them. They could not but be aware that they had seniors and contemporaries getting on perfectly well without courses.

They were highly critical of the department. They complained of unpunctuality, lack of preparation, overlapping between lectures, and administrative slips. They felt that if their teachers did not arrange their own organization well, they were unlikely to be able to teach good management to others.

They were surprised by the unconventional character of the teaching approach they were meeting for the first time – an approach, led by the new teachers, which laid an unexpected emphasis on non-directive methods, and attempted to draw students' attention to social and psychological elements in work situations by making some use of 'here-and-now' material in the classroom.

They felt that the teaching approach was often 'over-theoretical', and emphasized psychology and sociology at the expense of practical work. They were puzzled at the teachers' enthusiasm for analysis of the way in which technical problems arose, and apparent under-emphasis of the technical problems themselves; at what seemed to be the lack of direction in classes; at the efforts to talk about what was happening in the relationship between student and teacher; at the teachers' habit of making what seemed to be 'personal' remarks to them.

Part of the explanation for the discontent of the students was, we were sure, their dissatisfaction with themselves – they were, in a sense, blaming the teachers for being unable to do the impossible, to transform them through teaching into successful executives. At the same time, it was clear that there was some substance in many of their complaints – departmental administration was, in fact, often inefficient; the social aspects of the students' work situations were not being elucidated in a natural enough way by being allied to the technical discussions; too sudden a departure was being made from the conventional one-way delivery of material which students expected; and, when teachers first used unstructured group discussions or 'quasi-interpretative' methods, they sometimes confronted students with facts about their behaviour in a way that was challenging rather than helpful.

Studies of Firms

Our studies of firms showed that local managements attached limited importance to training. Even where the firms had their own training departments they did not show great enthusiasm for them. So far as external training organizations were concerned, though these were used, doubt existed about the contribition that could be made by outsiders. Each firm pointed to it own special production techniques and operational problems.

The executives we saw expressed special scepticism about the value of formal training in management or supervision; and repeatedly said that managers were born, not made.

They had an image of a technical college teacher as an educated and experienced person. But he was seen as closer to a school teacher than a university lecturer, and was expected to be a person of mediocre calibre. He was viewed as a member of a small and impotent organization closely bound by regulations. His time was not regarded as precious and he was thought to be over-theoretical.

The larger firms conceded that it was useful for them to have such departments as the Helmsley management department to provide classes for junior supervisory staff in 'methods study' and, to a lesser extent, in 'management' studies of the conventional type. But where they had promising staff of potential seniority they preferred to send them to study under specialists of greater proven experience and skill.

The position of smaller companies was rather different. While they needed advice on the organization and supervision of production, and their junior employees actively wished to remedy their deficiencies in general or technical education, their managements were hesitant to invest a significant proportion of resources in training.

In both the larger and smaller companies the local college was regarded as one among many organizations competing for a limited market of students. Few managers and supervisors had much knowledge of the Helmsley management department, or knew the names, qualifications, and experience of the staff.

It was clear that a pronounced gap existed between industrial firms and the department, and that the managements of those firms had low expectation of it. Where there was current contact, it was failing to inspire confidence. The managers did not feel that they understood the aims or methods of the department as explained to them or demonstrated by the new head and his colleagues. They thought that a discrepancy existed between the aims of the staff (in so far as these were understandable) and the practical competence they displayed. Like many of the students, they felt the preoccupations of the staff to be vague, abstract, 'over-psychological', and irrelevant to their needs. They related stories of students who complained that, instead of being given the instruction they required, they were subjected to 'personal' remarks about their behaviour.

STAFF RECEPTION OF FINDINGS

As these findings accumulated we reported them back to the staff. We commented in a general form, which did not reveal names of individual informants, on the attitudes of students and firms towards them and what they taught.

Our first attempt to convey critical information and help the staff to make constructive use of it was a failure. The information concerned a course we had been observing. At the meeting held to consider the written report we had prepared, the staff group said that our criticisms were overdone, that they were based on insufficient evidence, that the conclusions reached were merely matters of opinion, and that our judgement was not necessarily correct. They said that many of the faults pointed out were well enough known to them without further comment from us. They said they resented being treated like students having exercises corrected. They were worried about the possibility of the reports reaching a wider audience (especially our Institute colleagues) who could influence their careers. Unfavourable opinions might be formed of them on the basis of the reports.

We had refrained from any comment on the course during our observations, so that teachers had no way of knowing, before the receipt of this document, what we thought. There is no doubt that this error of judgement exacerbated the critical nature of the response.

Reactions to this first report were, however, not wholly unfavourable. One member pointed out that the research would be of little value if we only praised what we saw, and if the teaching group was prepared to accept nothing that was uncomplimentary.

Over the course of a series of meetings, discussion gradually moved from the overall reactions of the staff to our reports, towards the detailed points made in them. The activity of our joint research worker and teacher group became more task-oriented, with the meetings concentrating on how to improve subsequent action. So far as Mr. Hutton and I were concerned, we were helped to influence the movement in this direction by the comment of a colleague to the effect that the teachers and we were behaving like negotiators at a bargaining table, rather than as one set of people with an operational task and another set with an advisory task.

Hurt feelings remained on the staff side for some time and we continued to feel it necessary to justify our comments. But a greater degree of agreement was reached between staff and ourselves on the appropriateness of various types of teacher behaviour in different situations.

It was a major strain on the department staff to tolerate the criticism of themselves by firms and students, and to know that we thought much of this justified. Through our close contact with the teachers and their work context, we could understand some of their difficulties (unequal abilities of students, unreality of their demands, shortage of trained staff, opposition of colleagues, and so on). But we made it clear that we thought they could do more to improve matters than they were in fact doing.

The major strain for us was toleration of their ambivalence towards us. We felt rather like guests invited to dinner, who settle down to criticize their hosts and to authenticate the criticisms.

A substantial contribution to a constructive outcome of this early crisis was made by the fact that we showed ourselves prepared to be corrected. Even more important, we were ready to help to seek remedies for the defects we had commented on.

There were many subsequent occasions on which the staff questioned our judgement, corrected us, or disliked our findings or advice (and on which we corrected our information). But it became more or less accepted that we brought information (even unpopular information) into the department and commented on its practical implications, while the department made selective use of our knowledge, experience, and advice. And we had learned to voice our impressions while they were being formed, however tentative they might be, rather than let tension mount as staff waited for formal written statements.

The give and take can be illustrated from an incident that could in another atmosphere easily have proved catastrophic to our project. At one stage I passed a document to the principal before formal consent was given by the department. This arose through a misunderstanding between Mr. Richardson and myself. A member of the department said that this was proof of the risks to which staff exposed themselves in projects of this type. Mr. Richardson pointed out that it showed mainly that he and I could make mistakes. This view was accepted.

As the project progressed, tension slackened in relations between the older members of the department and ourselves. One important reason was that our growing knowledge of firms and students led us to the conclusion that the pace of innovation was too drastic, that the new staff members were introducing new teaching techniques before they had adequately mastered them, and that they needed to conserve much of what was positive and useful in the older, more conventional, tradition. When we made this clear, the older members of the department began to see us as 'objective' people, who would take a balanced view of a situation rather than side with one or other faction. Another major contribution to amicable relations came from the collaboration with me of Mr. Cook, the senior lecturer in the department, in a short study of the training needs of a firm that approached the department for help for its supervisory staff. During the course of this study Mr. Cook and I had much the same role with regard to the firm's staff as my Institute colleague and I had in our relations with the department staff. He and his colleagues were able to see even more clearly now that in the course of such an investigation one scrupulously respected individual confidences; concentrated on questions of structure, roles, and relationships rather than on individual personality or individual competence; and had as one's central aims the understanding of the organization, and the provision of help in the constructive use of this understanding.

THE POST OF TEACHER

Since many of the problems depended ultimately on what a full-time teacher could and could not do, we undertook a detailed analysis of the teacher's post as it was and could be. This was done mainly through repeated group discussions with the staff. After every two or three such discussions we prepared a set of notes which were further developed on the next occasion.

The teacher had to face the central problems common to all teaching about behaviour, i.e. the necessity for the student to begin to deal in an unfamiliar way with apparently familiar events, and to go further for explanation than physical fact and personal idiosyncrasy. It was especially difficult to re-orient the thinking of students accustomed to working with concrete objects.

There were added difficulties arising from the kinds of student attracted. While it was not part of the teacher's formal obligation to go beyond academic teaching in furthering the student's career, he knew that this would not be enough. He had constantly to devise teaching approaches which, while being generally helpful to the student, were within his own competence and legitimate within the college context. The distinction between education for management and attempted psychological therapy was at times difficult to draw. Yet the teacher dared not err, for fear of turning an educational establishment into a disguised psychiatric clinic, or of raising psychiatric problems for whose resolution he could not accept responsibility.

The teacher's discussions and negotiations with employers were often delicate. It was difficult for an industrial executive to explain, or for the teacher to understand, exactly what the employer or the students needed. Often the executive was operating from a base at which differences of opinion had not been adequately resolved. For the teacher to accept some of the requests made to him at face value would be unconstructive; he would be evading an issue merely for the sake of appearing helpful. While it was easier and safer to deal with the narrower, more specific, teaching problems with which help was formally requested, the situation discussed sometimes seemed to cry out for the more fundamental help he was anxious to give. If arrangements for such work were made the initiative would have to come from the firm, and the teacher would have to be quite sure in his own mind that he would be tackling something comfortably within his technical competence and within his terms of reference as a staff member of a technical college.

Sometimes the executive would become convinced that the teacher had little to offer. The unimpressive environment of the department, the novel views of several staff members, and their elaborate determination to clarify their roles often strengthened this impression.

The teachers tended to be over-anxious to show what they could do, and to try to prove that, despite limitations in their practical experience, they could be of value to the students and their employers. They often took inquiries too far from their point of departure and too fast into 'social science country'. This could only bewilder people who had come with what they had thought of as a highly concrete problem.

Support from the rest of the college was uneven. The members of the department who were newly appointed had types of background and outlook very different from those of many of their colleagues in other departments who were mainly occupied in teaching technological theories and skills. Their subjects were novel, and tended to encourage anxiety or defensive amusement. The determination of the department, and especially the head, to break away from conventional college work challenged the tradition of one-way delivery of lecture material as a method of instruction, the use of student numbers and certificates as criteria for successful teaching, the assumption that the passing on of knowledge and technique discharged the obligation of a teaching institution to its students.

From time to time other departments would approach the management department to collaborate with them, but difficulties often arose when this collaboration was about to be put into practical effect. It seemed as if the other departments were both intrigued by what the management department staff were doing and made apprehensive by it.

A distinct difference existed between what teachers in the department were formally required to do by the college and County authorities, and what they actually did or wanted to do. They spent less than the required proportion of hours in formal face-to-face teaching, but more in broader educational work. They were allowed too little time to become familiar with the work environments of students.

The difference between practical reality and formal requirement was on the whole well tolerated by the college principal and County Council authorities. Strains arose, however, because of unresolved ambiguities about formal duties and informal leeway, and because of the difficulties facing the staff in establishing new types of service, for which there existed few precedents and little public demand, and which offered little opportunity for the demonstration of spectacular short-term success.

We gained the impression that the staff were at times over-insistent in their attempts to get clarity of definition about what was being permitted to them. This was, we thought, largely because they wanted recognition of the worthwhileness of what they were doing, and were anxious to gain more active encouragement and positive sanction. There were, however, in our view, many occasions on which it would have been wiser to get on with the actual experimental work than to engage in attempts at clarification or in arguments with higher authorities that could constitute only distractions for the department or additional 'evidence' for the authorities that they had a deviant and obstreperous group on their hands.

Central difficulties stemmed from the threat of new emphases and developments to the efficiency of the established work and routines of the department. This was caused partly by over-ambition on the part of the staff. The department was planning for more work than was possible with existing staff, and the teachers lacked the training and experience necessary to do the work which they correctly diagnosed as necessary.

DEVELOPMENT OF THE DEPARTMENT'S WORK

We continued to pass on to the teachers selected material from our studies of the students, the firms, and themselves, and to discuss practical implications for current and projected work with industry. There was considerable sensitivity about many of the points raised, especially where these indicated, as they frequently did, a need for changes in staff behaviour.

But changes occurred in what both we and they considered a positive direction.

The department critically reviewed its teaching programme. It pruned those of its conventional management courses which appeared to confer paper qualifications rather than to develop managerial ability. It exercised greater discretion in the acceptance of students. Mainly through the use of guided group discussion, staff improved their techniques of teaching emotionally charged material. They made their teaching more practical by wide use of project methods. A tutorial system was instituted to personalize responsibility for students, and bring part-time teachers into closer contact with the full-time staff through more frequent consultations about students. Three new appointments were made, one being a replacement for Mr. Gray who left to take up an industrial appointment. The new teachers were Mr. Hunt, whose academic qualifications were in commerce and education, and who had experience in clinical psychology; Mr. Jenkins, who had a degree in history, and industrial experience in training and personnel selection; and Dr. Kaye, who was a specialist in sociological theory. To prevent a confusion of educational and quasi-therapeutic functions in the department, it was decided that Mr. Hunt would provide a formal career counselling service for students. He helped young men already in the department, or proposing to become students, to make realistic assessments of what they could and could not expect to gain from their studies. Mr. Jenkins, an experienced industrial executive, devoted much of his time during his first months to administrative needs, and the operating efficiency of the department was visibly improved.

It became clear that the department had to lower its sights in work with firms and to safeguard its core of conventional, acceptable work. The firms felt that it was trying to do too much too quickly. In some cases this reached a point where firms were discouraged from continuing with the department even in conventional work. Departmental plans over-estimated the amount and kind of work acceptable to firms and possible for staff in view of their skills and the nature of the administrative structure in which they were employed.

We worked with the staff towards the greater realization that they had to co-operate with firms in a way that showed they could tolerate circumscription of their efforts and develop new opportunities. This was best done on limited and well-defined tasks. The most suitable tasks, the department decided, would be 'training surveys', in which the department would study training needs with firms and report to them how far it could provide the necessary training, or advice on training, that was needed. (As previously mentioned, we designed and executed one such survey of a firm in collaboration with Mr. Cook, as a model for further efforts by the department on its own.)

The department sought to concentrate on the development of links with a relatively small number of firms. Apart from training surveys, some small-scale field research began and joint teaching programmes began to develop.

Through the very fact of our investigations, significant changes occurred in relations between the department and surrounding firms. Contact with us increased the willingness of firms to give the department research opportunities and to tolerate experimentation that was novel and sometimes confusing to them. At the same time we encountered a problem in the fact that the firms often became interested in us rather than in members of the department. They were sometimes disappointed that subsequent events involved them with the department and not the Institute. We had to point out that the department's members could not be expected to be ready-made specialists and would have to go through much of their learning with the firms.

Two or three of the firms became interested enough to suggest a meeting with teachers in the department and ourselves, to discuss existing relations between the college and firms, and the work that the department could most usefully undertake. We convened a one-day conference – to which representatives of examining institutions, the County Council, and the Ministry of Education were also invited – to discuss our findings and their implications. This was followed by another more action-oriented meeting convened by the chairman of the governing body of the college. At this meeting the chairman, the head of the department, and I, suggested that a development panel be formed between the department and a few representatives of local firms to consolidate and expand the direct links formed between them during the research. Members of the County Council education committee and of the college Board of governors seemed to resent the suggestion that something was lacking in relations with firms and that new arrangements were needed. Anxiety about the effectiveness of the college was, however, low enough to permit constructive suggestions to be made as to the exact functions and operations of the panel, and to enable members to arrange for representatives of firms, the department, and the college principal to present concrete proposals to the governing body.

A development panel was subsequently formed. Because firms and the department had inter-related needs, and because the staff offered to work immediately on concrete problems of the firms, the panel contributed to the growth of relationships of a more enduring quality between teachers and industrial employers, and provided opportunities for mutual learning and co-operative experimentation.

As they developed their plan for work with students and firms, and studied the criticisms which we voiced or reported, members of the department felt it would be an advantage to have more training in research and training techniques.

The head of the department asked whether we could arrange this advanced training at the Tavistock Institute. We agreed that this might help to increase the teachers' competence and the confidence of firms in what they could offer. We gave a course attended by all departmental staff, at which my colleagues and I led seminars on Institute projects and case conferences on problems brought.

Apart from such theoretical teaching, members of the department seemed to profit from the fact that they could observe at close range now Mr. Hutton and I, as social scientists based on an organization with a relatively established tradition, went about our work, and could evaluate with us the modes of approach we adopted.

REACTIONS OF COLLEGE AND COUNTY AUTHORITIES

We kept the County Council in touch with findings and developments through regular discussion of progress reports with the liaison committee, and through the official responsible for technical college education. On the whole the college and County atmosphere was favourable to experiment. But anxiety continued to be expressed lest we be unduly critical or make unrealistic recommendations, and lest the department be encouraged to do something irresponsible. Our studies brought problems to the focus of attention and it seemed at times as if we or the teaching staff were creating these problems.

It was difficult for college and County authorities to appreciate the full implication of our finding that traditional ways of work with students and firms were failing to meet the wants and needs of those for whose benefit they were intended. We pointed out that if the work was to be properly executed, staff would need more liberal interpretation, or relaxation, of many existing regulations. They would require greater freedom to provide experience for students and to work out appropriate training arrangements with firms.

It was naturally difficult for the County Council to make changes that might affect a number of departments in different colleges on the basis of the shown needs of one department. The acceptability of change was further retarded by the fact that the over-ambitious start of the department was damaging its established work.

In this situation it is surprising, not so much that the County Council and college did not accept all suggested innovations, as that they accepted and co-operated in as many as they did. That they did so was, in our opinion, largely owing to the unambiguous and elaborately manifest research conclusion that the precautions adopted to safeguard the investment of the taxpayer (i.e. rigorous definitions of hours of work, categories of work, types of approved teaching; and restrictions on research, experimenting, and consulting) were becoming constraints that threatened the purpose of the investment.

A situation had been created in which a teacher could conform to all the regulations and go through all the required motions without helping anyone. This was a cause of frustration to him and to the firms with which he sought to work. These concerns were much more flexible and adaptable than the college which, as a recipient of public funds, was preoccupied with carefully laid-down procedures that could be described and justified to ratepayers.

At the same time, the more successful parts of the experimental work were showing that if existing regulations were relaxed, if on-going work was realistically evaluated, and if the staff could grow in skill, it was possible even with the existing structure for the teaching group to make certain positive advances.

BRINGING THE PROJECT TO AN END

Towards the end of the project we announced a plan to taper off the work. We said that major emphasis would now be on the writing-up of the project and the clearing of documents with the department and County Council. We would have to reduce field work to a minimum. Meetings would be less frequent. The department should get used to the idea of a looser relationship. These ideas were acceptable in principle, but it was evident that the staff were reluctant to lose our active support and interest, and to accept the fact that the financial scope of the project necessitated its close. When it came to practical arrangements, it was with some difficulty that a programme was agreed upon which involved less contact. The staff, and particularly the department head, were eager to have us remain in close enough touch to see their new work, and to be able to report on improvements and to assess and evaluate changes. We emphasized that a major objective of the research would be frustrated if sufficient time were not left for the final writing of research reports.

The position gradually became stabilized, partly through our reiteration of the fact that field involvement at this stage could only sabotage the completion of a final report, and partly through the fact that appreciable developments were occurring in the department's work which were their own advertisement.

The main form of contact became meetings at which the final documents drafted by us were discussed before their communication to the principal and County Council.

By this stage it was noticeable that the staff were less concerned that anything indiscreet or critical might be said about them than interested in seeing that our findings would be presented in a way that would maximize their influence. We could make more candid comments by this time, as we were able to state not the bare fact that one activity or another was unsuccessful, but that progress had been made from one unsatisfactory position to another more satisfactory one.

In the final event all the main significant facts which we considered worth presenting about the department and its activities were reported, and the County Council, which, like the department and college, was by now familiar with our main conclusion, agreed without any restrictions to the publication of our findings.[1]

[1] I have nevertheless chosen in this case to conceal identities for the sake of consistency with the other cases.

PART II

THEORETICAL ANALYSIS

CHAPTER 4

THERAPEUTIC AND RESEARCH COMPONENTS OF THE WORK

I. THE PROVISION OF HELP

MY work had two foci. One was the provision of help to the organization – the therapeutic component; the other was the scientific use of the material to which access was gained – the research component. I shall deal first with the therapeutic component. This consisted of:

(i) The assembly and analysis of facts, and re-conceptualization of problems.
(ii) Redefining assumptions and expectations.
(iii) Participation in planning and action.
(iv) Introducing, monitoring, and evaluating innovations.

(i) *The Assembly and Analysis of Facts, and Re-conceptualization of Problems*

All three projects involved the systematic collection and analysis of information. In the case of the Helmsley project, the information was derived from the administration of questionnaires and intelligence tests to students; individual interviews and group discussions with them, with business men, and educational administrators; classroom observations; and staff discussions. In the case of the Davidson project, case studies were made of production departments; systematic descriptions of key roles were built up; and group discussions and individual interviews were conducted throughout. In the hospital project, the collection of information was deliberately confined to group discussions with the main categories of staff and with the project committee.

The importance of fact-finding in this work can, however, be over-stated. For one thing, the facts I collected were often new only to me – the organization knew about them already. For another, the mere collection of facts may well be found to give little help; indeed it has been shown in experimental work that an individual's capacity for making sound judgements about complex situations may even be impaired by providing him with a mass of data (which he believes should be relevant) unless he understands quite clearly how it influences or should influence his behaviour. Thirdly, when boiled down to 'findings', the types of factual conclusions or leads for action with which a social consultant emerges are apt to seem obvious, common sense or trivial. This is partly because people know many truths 'intuitively' and partly because they retain simultaneously several broad theories about cause and effect, one of which may well be supported by research.

Often it was the process of analysis, the redefinition of the problem, the character of the material mustered, the weights which different items were given, which provided the most help for the administrators. These did not necessarily provide fresh answers or conclusions, but contributed more usefully and lastingly to the deepening and extension of capacity for judgement, to the birth of new conceptions of how human problems should be defined, and to the clarification and explication of the logical basis for conclusions already suspected.

Perhaps more important to the administrators than 'factual' findings was the *manner* in which my colleagues and I defined and re-conceptualized the problems with which we were presented; made existing assumptions explicit and examined their validity; assessed which of the contradictory and equally 'obvious' conclusions about situations were in fact true; illuminated the social and psychological forces at work, accepting feelings and attitudes as social facts which had to be included in any overall appreciation; and drew attention to role and culture conflicts previously defined wholly as interpersonal issues. Indeed, it would be legitimate to regard much of what was done in the three projects as a special sort of training experience for administrators, based on sociological and psychological expertise.

(ii) *Redefining Assumptions and Expectations*

The assumptions about human behaviour, on which directorates operate, commonly under-estimate the extent to which people are willing to take responsibility and to make their resources available to the organizations to which they belong. In all three cases my presence and method of work increased confidence that colleagues could agree on a common set of organizational objectives and adopt them on their own. Looking back, I should say that I communicated my belief in this possibility by beginning in each case by finding key groups with which I could concentrate my work. Although there existed at the same time a central person to whom I acknowledged a special responsibility – the managing director of the Davidson Company, the director of the research unit, the head of the management department – the relationship with the key group of organizational leaders conveyed my belief that they had unused capital available to them as a collectivity.

The established expectations of groups of staff concerning particular colleagues often functioned to restrict the contribution they made. The expectations had become a set of self-fulfilling prophecies. A collusive system had developed, for instance, between the Davidson Board and Mr. Davis, in which each party expected (and obtained) less goodwill, help, and flexibility from the other than was in fact possible. To some extent I think the same was true of the ways in which the medical staff regarded the senior nursing staff of the James Division, and the newly appointed social scientists and the engineers regarded each other in the first phases of the work with the Helmsley management department. My impression is that in each case my work brought the established systems of reciprocal expectations into question, and enabled participants to set slightly higher standards for each other in a way which called forth not only a more co-operative atmosphere but also somewhat better contributions.

(iii) *Participation in Planning and Action*

As an outsider the consultant provides a relatively objective and independent viewpoint. I brought an extra mind of a different sort to the problems of the groups with which I worked, and information about the way other organizations tackle similar or related problems. From my general training in social science and practical experience with organizations I was able to contribute ideas for solving operational problems of selection, appraisal, communication, and training; and for collecting information about the character of the environment.

My presence helped the groups to be more objective, as it provided them with an opportunity to project themselves into my position to try to see themselves as I saw them. This is the complement of the insight which derives from the consultant's capacity to project himself into the position of members of the group.

My interest and the involvement themselves acted as forces helping the groups to achieve their objectives. The very fact that I was prepared to enter into a relationship with the groups suggested to them that change was possible. This combined with their feelings about my expertise in social psychological matters to permit them to work on problems they would otherwise have had to ignore as too difficult or too dangerous. They were helped by my apparent willingness to tolerate solutions at the level that was really possible for them, however defective these might be by ideal criteria.

In the case of the Helmsley and Davidson work, the project groups had the active help of certain of my colleagues as well as myself. They helped in the collection and analysis of information, in first-hand discussion of its policy implications, and in matters of training, appraisal, and selection. But there was still another sense in which client groups were helped to form policy, i.e. by the fact that we could open routes for them to resources which they did not know beforehand or which they would not normally realize were available for their purposes. One example of this was the decision that could be made by the

Davidson firm to offer certain existing and prospective members of the company consultations with clinical psychologists designed to help them to consider their future careers.

There were many concrete changes with which we assisted the Helmsley group: to develop a policy of greater concentration in the range of firms with which collaborative work was attempted and in the range of students to be trained; to introduce counselling with students, training surveys, and a development panel with firms; and to select and train their own staff. We helped the Davidsons to form a long-term personnel policy that would contribute towards the ends of the organization and separate these from familial needs; to deal through counselling and consultation with the personal problems that this posed for existing senior executives and their young relatives; to introduce more objective procedures for judging prospective entrants to the firm; and to select those entrants from among a variety of applicants. In the hospital case I helped the James Division to set up an institution (meetings of the three senior administrators) for considering policy and assessing the way the work was going, and illustrated a form of procedure (group discussion with representative groups of staff) that brought relevant information to attention.

(iv) *Introducing, Monitoring, and Evaluating Innovations*

All three projects involved some changes in and by the project groups. There were shifts in perceptions and definitions of problems, in the contexts in which particular questions were examined, in the way in which decisions were taken, in the character of organizational decisions, and in the manner and timing of their execution. These changes can be summed up in the statement that in the course of each project there was some movement by each group towards the discovery of its primary task and towards the establishment of better means for attaining this.

My colleagues and I were partly responsible for these changes, to which we contributed information, frames of reference, moral support, experience, 'feedback' from the environment, ideas, and suggestions. We also helped through providing formal and informal occasions for the review and evaluation of new institutions. In the Helmsley case, the introduction of student counselling, and attempts to improve departmental administration and teaching methods, were regularly reviewed with the staff group as a basis for further improvement. In the Davidson case, we jointly reviewed the ways in which the newly innovated appraisal, selection, and training procedures contributed to the solution of some problems and raised others; after the management committee had been functioning for some months, my colleagues and I reviewed with the managing director and with the Board the ways in which it was functioning, its uses, and what we considered to be its abuses.

In the case of the hospital project, there was one structural innovation – the constitution of a project committee consisting of the research unit director, the chief of clinical service, and the head nurse. We also introduced a method of receiving information and helping operations, in the form of group discussions with staff. It was understood from the beginning that we were conducting in the latter, and in my work with the staff groups and the project committee, a form of experimental innovation that would bear repetition and development by another social consultant if it proved helpful. For this reason, every meeting with the project committee, and especially the last, carefully went over the record of what had been done and considered what was helpful and needed institutionalization.

Comparison with Psychotherapy

The objectives and procedures that have been described inevitably raise the issue of their similarity to, or difference from, long-term psychotherapy.

In both cases there is one party with a problem, another obliged to try to help to deal with the problem, and a protracted professional relationship between the two that permits the collection of information which the party with the problem would in other contexts regard as his own business. There is sanctioned access to private data. Interaction is geared towards the collection and study of such information, and its communication to the client in such a way that he will arrive at a fuller understanding of his own problems and be helped to use that understanding constructively. The mere communication of information is not enough and provision is made for the repeated working over of material so that its implications can be fully absorbed and used.

In both cases explicit cognizance is taken of the presence of the therapists in the field, and the character of the relationship the client forms or tries to form with the therapist becomes an instrument of study and treatment.[1]

In both cases the therapist must be able to estimate motives and capacities; the probable outcome of conflict; the amount of stress that can be borne in the receipt of unfavourable information or clearer understanding; readiness to receive communications which, wrongly timed, would have a retrogressive rather than a progressive effect; and the likelihood that anxieties aroused will result in positive effort.

In both cases a successful outcome constitutes, or is accompanied by, the freeing of resources within the client not previously accessible to him in the pursuit of the objectives he professes.

At the same time the processes described in the three case studies differed in many ways from psychotherapeutic relationships as commonly structured and experienced. They differed in objective; in financial and practical arrangements made between the parties; in the content of the work; in the frames of reference used and in the extent to which attempts were made to share these with clients; in the use made of clinical understanding; and in the problems of responsibility posed.

Objectives.—The objective was not to change individuals or relieve them of pain. If the activities of the organizations had become more successful, the work could have been regarded as achieving its aims even with no change at all in the amount of happiness or unhappiness of individual members.

Nor was the objective the therapy of relationships – there were no attempts to improve relationships for their own sake. In some cases relationships were improved, in the sense that people got on better with each other, in others they were not.

[1] See Chapter 5, Section I.

This was incidental to the task of helping the group to function more effectively.

At the same time I did not see my task to be the improvement of efficiency in any immediate sense. In each case there were numerous occasions on which immediate problems could have been 'solved', in the sense of a rational or effective answer being found to an emergency. But it often happened that the longer the issues were kept open and mulled over, the more evident it became that although these measures would have dealt with some immediate problem they would have expressed opportunistic values, which might eventually have damaged the capacity of the directorate to mobilize the spontaneous commitment of the staff to the enterprise. It seemed to me on these occasions that my function was rather to help the leaders of the organizations or part-organizations with which I worked to resist the temptation to make quick and convenient decisions, and to balance these against the likely long-term consequences of their actions.

Arrangements between the parties.—The relationship was one between two organizations, not between two individuals nor between an organization and an individual.

The organization did not necessarily make a financial sacrifice, as is usually involved where psychotherapy is concerned.

The amount of work executed, and its duration, did not depend primarily upon the state of the client, his income, or preparedness to pay. The educational and the hospital projects would have ended at the same date whether or not the services of the department or the research unit had improved. In these cases, accordingly, the question of criteria for an appropriate moment to attenuate the relationship did not arise in the same way as in psychotherapy. It did, however, in the Davidson case, where the amount and character of our context were variable and flexible, and determined, within a stable overall understanding, more or less on a consultation-to-consultation basis.

Therapeutic work was interlaced with service operations (training for the Helmsley group, selection for the Davidsons) which had their own independent validity and usefulness.

The professional relationship was not as isolated as therapy is from ordinary, conventional, social and convivial relationships. While psychotherapy is usually attempted in a context deliberately insulated from the disturbances of the external world, the work described took place out in the open social world. I preferred not to make close friends of my clients – on the grounds that this would reduce the objectivity of my judgements in work with them, and would exacerbate questions of whether greater intimacy with one person or another was influencing my findings or recommendations. But I often joined them in meals during the working day, would not avoid convivial occasions to which they and I were invited, organized events (conferences, selection procedures) which involved them, and sought accounts of experiences with them and opinions on their behaviour from third parties (students, potential employees).

Content of work.—In psychotherapy the therapist places emphasis upon the ways in which the patient perceives social reality rather than upon the reality itself. The interest of the therapist and the treatment he gives his patient are concentrated on the latter's characteristic, personalized responses to the outer world.

In the three projects described a good deal of attention was directly focused on the external environments of the organizations. 'Reality' or 'objective' information on the environments was collected for presentation to clients and consideration with them.

The projects sometimes went beyond description to change the environments of the client organizations. Psychotherapy, by contrast, usually changes only the 'internal' world of the patient and has little effect on his external environment, except to the extent that people behave differently to the client as he changes and that he may seek out fresh types of environment. The projects described in some cases made substantial alteration in external working relationships of the client organizations considered as wholes – e.g. in the Helmsley case, through presenting information and recommendations to college and County Council authorities, through conferences and less formal interaction with people connected with the department; and in the Davidson case, by helping to present the company in a revised light during the processes of recruiting and selecting new staff.

In both therapy and collaborative research the object is to help the client to overcome problems. The therapist projects himself into the psychology of the client, and tries to empathize with him, to see the world from his point of view. In the projects described I tried to see the difficulties of my clients from their points of view but, in addition, in so far as these difficulties related to external social circumstances and I could contribute to altering these, I did so.

The work described contained an active advisory and counselling component absent from most long-term psychotherapy. In psychotherapy the individual learns to find his own way; in social consultancy the consultant frequently points the way. The diagnoses are more explicit and the comments more directive.

Frames of reference.—The main theoretical frame of the work was sociological and social-psychological. It was also derived to a significant extent from the psychology of the individual, but was not primarily centred on this as it is in the case of psychotherapy. Thus I would usually be thinking in terms of the character of the situations in which people were involved rather than in terms of the psychological functioning of each individual.

I tried to share this viewpoint, as much as I could and as explicitly as I could, with respondents. My impression is that I shared my frames of reference, orientation, concepts, and ways of looking at situations much more than a psychotherapist does. The latter is less concerned with what lies outside the individual, and it is not his task (as I conceived my own partly to be) to 'educate' the client so that he is able to take a more tolerant and sophisticated standpoint in handling others for whom he has responsibility and to improve their environment.[1]

The use made of clinical understanding and interpretations.[2] No interpretations of unconscious motivations or associa-

[1] Psychotherapy may have this incidental effect but it is not its purpose.

[2] I do not mean to imply in this section that my use of clinical understanding was optimal, given the situations in which I was placed. I have tried merely to give as good account as I can of the sort of things I did and said or attempted to do and say.

tions of ideas were made in terms of internal psychological dynamics at the individual level of personal therapy. (I use the term 'interpretation' here to mean the making conscious of what is unconscious in the mental functioning of an individual, so that he can gain an increased insight into consistent elements in his behaviour, and thus be helped to behave in a different way.)

I (or, when others were involved, we) tried to avoid making remarks to respondents at a level more personal than that of ordinary exchanges between colleagues, though because of our special responsibilities towards respondents and our (relative) independence from their organizations, we were often more candid as critics.

There were occasions in all three projects when I made interpretations in terms of more immediate group behaviour, i.e. of 'here and now' phenomena occurring while I was present, though on the whole I kept these to the minimum I thought necessary for the group to be helped with its problems. One occasion was within the Davidson project, when I gave my opinion at a meeting of the Board that our discussion of a Board member about to emigrate was a facet of the uneasiness of the relationship between that member and the other young director about the issue of which of them would ultimately succeed to the managing directorship.

In dealing with both individuals and groups I avoided making 'transference' interpretations, i.e. remarks about their feelings towards me and my work which would have included elements not fully conscious to respondents or displaced from other real and fantasy relationships. I thought that to do so would have been likely to introduce a dependence on me, or an intensity of feeling towards me, that I could not handle within the project, or to divert respondents from their main task to a substitute task, i.e. the examination of interaction with me. However, I carefully observed behaviour and attitudes towards me, so that I could make inferences from this that would be helpful to the work, and sometimes voiced these inferences at some later stage. To take a simple instance, I often voiced my opinion after observing exaggerated dependence on me that the fate of the project depended far less on my personal contribution than on how much respondents were prepared to learn and to do for themslevs.

I frequently made what may perhaps be described as quasi-interpretative comments to individuals and groups, more usually the latter, in terms of the consequences of their present behaviour for their organizations, for themselves, or for their professed aims. For example, I made my view plain to research unit members that if they continued to emphasize the negative views of themselves held by the hospital, and to blame difficulties on each other rather than take collective responsibility, they would be provided with a rationale for lack of research achievement and would be inhibited in their research productivity. I based such comments largely on my estimation of what constructions would spontaneously be put by others on the behaviour of the group, a basis which had to depend in turn partly on my own perception of the group's motivation. Thus I conveyed my opinion to the Davidson Board members that if they continued to exclude colleagues outside the family from the main dining-room those colleagues would assume that they did not mean what they said about opening up the firm.

I have said above that no individual interpretations were made. At the same time individuals certainly drew conclusions about themselves and their personal contributions to what were discussed as organizational or small-group phenomena on occasions such as those described. Inevitably they made inferences of personal significance. Secondly, the type of work, the concepts used, and repeated 'confrontations' with objectively presented descriptions of the environment encouraged (or obliged) members of each group to extract a degree of understanding which was more or less personal to them. It was inevitable that individuals would from time to time reconsider aspects of their behaviour as they became increasingly aware of opinions about them or of the impact of their behaviour. My colleagues and I tried controlling our own behaviour through our insight into ourselves, and this too resulted in some degree of 'self-analysis' by each research group.

It is possible that this approach makes the individual if anything more anxious than does psychotherapy, which entails an exploration of himself. Although therapy makes a client anxious, the therapist helps him to conquer that state of mind by exploring its nature. Communication of the nature of the outside world also makes the individual client of the social consultant personally anxious, but he receives help from the researcher only with the overt efforts he may make to deal more realistically with external reality; he is not helped in exploring the nature of his anxiety.

Problems of responsibility.—Social consultants and therapists have essentially similar responsibilities to society at large, to clients, and to their colleagues. But the task of the social consultant is complicated by the fact that his 'client-centred' responsibilities characteristically cover both individuals and an organization. Situations inevitably arise where it is difficult to reconcile the interests of an organization and of individual members. Problems may arise, for instance, where a key member of the organization confides to the consultant his intention to act in some way which is prejudicial to the organization. Or the consultant may become aware of some aspect of the functioning of that member which would be to his detriment if communicated to his employers, but which it would be desirable for them to know. While the consultant is probably morally bound to put the organization first – because his contract is with it, because the interests and welfare of more people are involved – he has to deal with the individual in a way consistent with the concern he must show for everyone with whom he has a professional therapeutic relationship and consistent with his wider social responsibilities.

There are some ways of reducing the possibility of such conflicts. One is for the consultant to make explicit to everyone the fact that the organization and its task have priority. Another is to attempt a separation between social consulting and professional counselling. It is often extremely difficult or impossible, in practice, to avoid personal communications made in the course of an organization-centred conversation with an individual, but the employment of a colleague for consultations of a more personal character serves a symbolic as well as a practical function in this respect. Discrepancies in the role of the consultant, deriving from the dual character of his responsibilities to organizations and individuals, are reduced where the organization acts justly towards its individual members and in full awareness of the wider consequences of considerate and inconsiderate behaviour towards them. It is, of course, part of the consultant's task to keep these matters under consideration. But there are many occasions on which the social consultant finds difficulty in ordering his responsibilities, feels the lack of traditional solutions of a more established occupation, and has to devise his own solution from first principles.

II. THE RESEARCH COMPONENT

Considered as a way of learning about organizational life, the approaches adopted in the three cases conferred certain unique opportunities, but simultaneously posed their own difficulties and carried their own limitations.

The Granting of Access

The method of work solved the problem of access that dogs empirical sociological study of contemporary society.

To understand the behaviour of organizations it is usually helpful and sometimes essential to undertake field studies, i.e. the first-hand observation of social events in the milieu and at the times when these actually occur. This necessity derives from the complexity of organizational behaviour, from the limitations of uninformed reflection, and from the need to check and elaborate under natural conditions such observations on stimulated social life as can practically and ethically be made in the laboratory.

Access to positions from which study may be undertaken is, however, difficult to obtain in Western society except in the investigator's own organization, where his study is bound to be grossly distorted by his personal standpoint and interests.

One important group of organizations – business firms – exclude observers largely because they see their effectiveness as depending on keeping competitors as ignorant as possible of their operations and plans. But even organizations which do not see their fate as dependent on confidentiality do not normally welcome observers. There are many reasons for this.

One obvious reason is that observers are felt to get in the way. More important, observation implies the possibility of comparisons that can challenge the rightness and inevitability of existing practices.

Much that occurs when people work together is painful, and those concerned are reluctant to have their discomfort witnessed or publicized. One likes to keep to a minimum the people who see or know one's personal conflicts, setbacks, and defeats.

A further inhibiting factor is the understandable though unrealistic anxiety that the act of making social and personal behaviour explicit may destroy the capacity for that behaviour, as in the classic case of the centipede who, when asked which leg he put forward first, thereafter found himself unable to walk.

Equally or more important among these barriers to the first-hand observation of organizational life is the centrality in our culture of the value of privacy in certain spheres of personal and institutional behaviour. These include work situations as well as domestic life. Unnecessary or frivolous violation of these areas constitutes an attack on a whole system of liberal ethics at the heart of which lies respect for the human personality and the maintenance of the maximum freedom in behaviour. That freedom includes freedom from observation of behaviour in private spheres where there is no prior reason for believing that the behaviour is such as to damage the society. Since our ethical system is embedded in ourselves as well as in inanimate objects, infringement of that system is an attack on the self. It could be argued that freedom of scientific inquiry should be allowed to transcend freedom from observation. But this argument is rendered less potent by the consideration that a social science which is to subserve human purposes is unlikely to be able to do so if in the process of gathering its data it attacks the very values on whose support its mandate is based.

In one approach commonly used to overcome the problem of access the research worker selects his topic for investigation, decides where he can carry out his field study, enters the field with little or no disclosure of his identity and purpose, and carries out his programme; he then withdraws, writes his report, and publishes it with such withholding or disguising of the data as he thinks expedient in the interests of the people studied or of himself. One obvious limitation to this approach is that the number of roles the observer can assume is closely limited. For instance, he can rarely assume a role that will lead him to the inner life of the organization. Working in his own society, and with people with whom he cannot but identify himself, he will feel uncomfortable about his concealment. The anxiety and guilt he experiences may well reduce or distort what he observes, and limit the range and depth of observations he will feel able to report. Serious ethical and professional objections can be made to this mode of operation. The investigator manipulates his subjects into a position where, not knowing his ulterior motive for entering a relationship with them, they are induced to enter that relationship on a false basis. It is difficult to justify entry into the private spheres of others where those whose privacy is to be infringed have been tricked into participation, have not been given the opportunity to suspend their rights voluntarily, and will receive no benefits from that infringement. This procedure is especially suspect where it can be argued, as in this case, that substantially the same information can be obtained by less dubious means. Furthermore, where one investigator has obtained his information through what is regarded as a sophisticated form of 'spying', others are almost certain to be carefully sought out and excluded, and the profession as a whole is apt to be discredited.

Alternatively, it is possible for the investigator openly to define the problem and the area to be studied, and take his research into the public area. He seeks the permission of the appropriate authorities for the right of access to the groups to be studied and undertakes to submit his report for permission to publish, but remains in intention and as much as possible in practice a passive observer. This mode of approach is both ethical and productive. It has the limitation, however, that the observer tends to be excluded from the inner councils of the leaders of the organization because they see little overlap between his interest and objectives and their own, and do not expect a return from him. He must confine most of his observations to matters of more peripheral concern to them. His anxiety about the fact that he is an outsider withholding knowledge and potentially useful advice, and that information is withheld from him, can also impair his observations.

In a third type of approach, that on which this book is based, the prospect of help is exchanged for the research opportunity. It was an explicit part of the contract with the organizations studied that attempts would be made to give them help with some of their problems. This gave me access to situations from which I would otherwise have been barred, and enabled me to stay in the field long enough to get a grasp of the very complex problems involved.

The Quality of the Relationship with Respondents

My acceptance of the role of social consultant implied a double type of professionalism from which it followed that the general character of my relations with respondents differed significantly from those usually existing between social investigators and the people they study. In many respects my role improved the quality of the data collected.

Investigation of contemporary society is based largely on a tradition of opposition to existing social arrangements and of attempts to draw attention to the unfortunate lot of those alienated from common benefit by poverty, race membership, distance from political power, and so on. While the individuals or groups from whom the data are directly derived rarely suffer from the fact of investigation, the research worker discharges his social responsibilities by fulfilling his obligations towards the larger society, to posterity, or to the wider categories of people to whom his respondents belong, rather than towards the respondents directly. A separate, though overlapping, type of investigation has attempted to discharge its social obligations through substantive or methodological contributions to scientific knowledge.

In the social consulting model, the investigator holds himself responsible not only to the wider society (or to his science) but also to the respondents themselves. Apart from any concern he may have with social causes and with method, he undertakes to do the best he can for respondents in the situation in which he finds them, to help them on from where they are to where they might practically and ethically attempt to go. The investigator does not try to divorce himself from them either by using them to indict the society or by maintaining a position of ethical neutrality about their endeavours. He accepts the fact that the institutions they operate have been granted a social validity which is not in question during the currency of his work.

In undertaking my work as a social consultant I entered the same moral order as my respondents, helping them to maintain what was positive in their situation and to alter what was negative. I made my knowledge, technical skills, and personal resources available to them, and gained a demonstrable, comprehensible, and clearly legitimized right to have theirs made available to me. They were co-operative in the highest degree because they were not being treated as objects for manipulation, as sources of information, or merely as means to a wider end. As it was in their interests as well as in mine that I should understand their situation fully, they helped me actively, and constantly checked and elaborated my observations.

For my part, being obliged to appreciate the viewpoint of the administration and to place this side by side with my own viewpoint, I learned more about their situation.

My responsibilities forced me to take cognizance (even though often somewhat crudely) of all the main forces in the field susceptible to my, or the respondents', perceptions, and of the relations between these. Especially when changes were attempted, and barriers and resistance encountered, I learned what maintained their organization in one state rather than another and what inhibited new developments. I do not think I could have learned so much if I had been less committed to help or in less intimate interaction with my respondents.

As there was no employment of subterfuge or concealment, and as I was not observing respondents for a secret reason or one which they did not share, I did not feel the embarrassment which social investigators commonly experience about watching or disturbing others. I was released from certain customary inhibitions regarding the invasion of privacy by an outside person. This model of work can increase the capacity of the investigator to observe, by reducing the anxiety and guilt associated with non-reciprocal social transactions.

While my involvement had its own costs in terms of loss of objectivity, I was brought close to my material through constant interaction with the people concerned. Where, in the past, I have assumed the more conventional role of silent observer, I have felt myself an all-purpose object for the projection of anxieties of a persecutory character. In the cases described in the book I was rather more like a new type of colleague.

Disadvantages and Difficulties

In discussing the research contributions that are possible within the types of work described, it would be useful to distinguish the Helmsley project from the two others. The Helmsley project had formal research objectives as well as operational and advisory aims. A great deal of material was collected in much the same way as would have been the case in any similar piece of research on the relations of a work group and of an educational organization to their environments. Some of the results were expressed in terms relevant to general theoretical sociological questions as well as to current operational issues. On the other hand, the research-therapy balance tilted in favour of the latter because of the preoccupation of both the research team and the departmental staff with the operational problems of the organization, with some probable loss to the explicit scientific contribution that might otherwise have been made.

In the two other projects the main objectives were therapeutic, and any scientific contributions that emerged had to be regarded as incidental to the main purpose. Though the work frequently had significance for an important theoretical problem and provided unusual opportunities for observation of, or participation in, the relevant processes, these opportunities could not be exploited to the full for scientific purposes. Helping a directorate which is undergoing a crisis in relations with another individual or group in the organization is, for instance, a different matter from formulating hypotheses about the limits of latitude that a directorate will permit and formally testing these through a range of situations.

Thus, in some degree in the third project and more drastically in the others, the scientific contribution – in the sense of the addition to a formal body of principles and knowledge about organizations in relation to their environments – was limited by the existence of an alternative, therapeutic objective, and by the conditions of work which this objective imposed.

In work of this type the investigator finds it difficult to study any problem except the one preoccupying his respondents. His choice of problem is restricted, and this makes it difficult for him, even over a period of years, to execute a sustained programme of research on one topic or to pursue a research interest through to a logical conclusion. He is lucky indeed if he can find a sequence of sufficiently similar or related problems in comparable organizations that will make systematic comparison possible. Nor can he make the most of his opportunities for access. Not knowing what will come up, he cannot formulate the relevant theoretical problem beforehand in the most fruitful way.

The risk of 'unrepresentativeness', common to all case studies, is underlined by the willingness of the respondents to have themselves and their organizations studied, by the intimacy that grows between organization and consultant, and by the fact that, by definition, the organization will change through his presence.

Once the work is in motion he forgoes much of his freedom of choice in regard to the order, the timing, and the conditions under which his data will appear. And he cannot isolate and control these in a way that would make possible the checking of his conclusions by other investigators in other organizations. It is, moreover, easy for him to be diverted even from those research interests with which he started by the urgencies of problems within the organization.

A certain loss of objectivity occurs through the fact that a high degree of emotional identification with the respondents and the activities in which they are engaged becomes inevitable. However well trained the investigator, this is likely to distort what he perceives and will wish to report. This is one reason why it is prudent to build into social consultancy projects an arrangement for regular review of the work by at least one uninvolved colleague.

Where payment is received from the client organization, loss of objectivity may also occur for a different reason. The way in which the organization handles the question of payment (questions, argument, delay, over-generosity, and so on) often gives the social consultant an indication of how the client feels about his work at any given time. But if the payment forms a significant proportion of his income, the consultant is bound to meet situations where he is tempted to compromise between his need for information and his need to avoid prejudicing his relationship with his client.

The research limitations placed on the work by the introduction of therapeutic objectives and a measure of financial dependence on clients are, of course, shared with medical clinicians. Those placed on the work by observing human beings in their own environments are shared with anthropological field workers. In both spheres, the fact of using single cases and lack of control over the timing of the events which are of interest and the conditions under which they occur, have not prevented the emergence of richly suggestive models of behaviour, which have contributed a unique understanding of the ways in which different facets of personality and of community life interlock, and oppose, support, and balance each other. It is a contribution of this character in the field of organizational study that I believe the social consultancy method will eventually be able to make. I doubt very much, however, if it will be able to make that contribution unless a research aim remains one of its explicit components, and unless a separate exercise is undertaken with each major field study in order to relate it as specifically as possible to a formal body of knowledge. In practical terms, this means that practical working relationships must be maintained with other social scientists working in a more academic atmosphere and by more conventional (and rigorous) methods, so that social consultants will be obliged continuously to share their conclusions and concepts, to test, refine, and reformulate them, in a way that will benefit not only their own services to their clients but also their colleagues and their discipline.

CHAPTER 5

REGULARITIES AND PRINCIPLES IN SOCIAL CONSULTANCY

THE previous chapter distinguished the therapeutic from the research component of the three projects and discussed the character, advantages, disadvantages, and problems of the three case studies viewed first as therapy and then as research. The question inevitably arises in connection with this double-focused approach of the extent to which it is, or can become, an established method of work for some social scientists, that is, a method of which the component principles can be identified, communicated, and transmitted. If those components cannot be identified, then the value of case studies of the type described consists in the benefits accruing to the project groups and in the experience gained by the investigator; their contribution to social science is no more than literary. If the component principles can in fact be identified, communicated, and transmitted, then we have the elements of a profession that can be developed and practised as a form of environmental mental health work, and can possibly make a systematic contribution to knowledge through providing a means of examining organization life.

This chapter accordingly sets out to provide tentative answers to the following questions:

I To what extent can regularities be identified in the type of work described in the three projects?

II To what extent can appropriate methods of work be identified and what are the implications of these methods for the social consultant?

III What sorts of preparation are most appropriate for social consultancy?

I. REGULARITIES IN THE DEVELOPMENT OF THE RELATIONSHIP BETWEEN THE ORGANIZATION AND THE SOCIAL CONSULTANT

Variations in the three Cases

It will be recalled that my role and my relationship with the group requesting help were not identical in the three cases described. The conditions under which that help was given varied greatly with respect to the relative emphasis given to operational ends and to research; the number of research workers involved; the duration and intensity of field contact; the position of the requesting group within its own wider structure; the way the cost of the work was borne; the amount of prior social and psychological sophistication possessed; and the early expectations of the character and amount of help to be given.

The relationship with the Helmsley group was in the context of a long-term research project. The production of descriptive field material and of conclusions based on this had precedence over the advisory, operational component of the work, though it was understood that there would be such a component. Emphasis in the industrial project was almost entirely operational, and every investigation that was conducted was a means to a practical end. The research unit study was similarly operational in purpose, though the atmosphere of my work was one favourable to clinical and academic study, and my respondents had some interest in the technicalities of my approach. This study was not on a level with the other two, which were both long and detailed studies extending over two years or more; it was an attempt at something much more limited – an appreciation with a sub-unit of an organization of the most conspicuous facets of its functioning accessible to observation by, or communicable to, a trained external observer; it was primarily a consulting operation.

The Helmsley project was a team effort on which two of us were engaged more or less full-time over two years. The main work on the industrial project took place over a similar period, but the extent of my involvement was much more variable – often I did not see the Davidsons for months at a time. In this case I led the work, but constantly had the advice of colleagues, and several times was assisted by them in the field. The study of the research unit was very brief; it was concentrated over about six weeks and as I was out of London I had virtually no help from colleagues.

The projects differed significantly in the fact that the Davidson and research group projects were requested by the group directing the organization which was the unit of study, while the Helmsley project involved a wider formal structure and a wider set of relationships than those of the management department which had made the original request.

Only in the case of the Davidsons did the cost of the work fall on the group requesting it. The Helmsley project was financed by the Department of Scientific and Industrial Research, and the research unit project by the organization providing funds for the unit.

The amount of sociological and psychological sophistication of the three requesting groups varied considerably. The Helmsley group consisted partly of social scientists, and the research unit was familiar with social research and research workers; no such contact had been experienced before by the Davidsons.

The Helmsley group knew that the work with them would last two years and, alongside the stated formal objectives of the project, assumed that there would be a considerable concentration on their interpersonal relations and expected me to adopt a predominantly interpretative procedure, much like that described by Jaques (1951) in *The Changing Culture of a Factory*. Subsequent reflection inclines me to the view that one unstated objective of the work was also to gain formal contact with the Tavistock Institute, which the department looked to for guidance in much that it hoped to do. The formal approach of the Davidsons to the Institute was for help with what was probably assumed to be a single selection procedure. Their immediate readiness to describe the fuller circumstances surrounding the selection problem, and their interest in utilizing the full range of services of the Institute once they knew them, indicated the existence of a keenly felt need for help in making a crucial set of changes. In the case of the hospital project it was at first only the head of the research unit who wanted my help. This was envisaged as a couple of days of contact with his staff and an expression of a view to him on his organization. This changed to a longer and more intricate piece of work when his two key senior colleagues became involved, and I clarified with the three the basis on which I could make a contribution to their efforts and what that contribution might be. They took what was to them a new and unexpected opportunity.

The fact that there were these differences between the three projects drew my attention the more vividly to the uniformities of process observable during the various phases of my relationships with the requesting group. It is with those uniformities rather than with the differences that this chapter is concerned, though there will be references to the points at which I noticed significant differences.

Minimum Conditions within the Organization

Work of the type described cannot be set in motion unless the organization contains leading members who realize that a problem exists and that there is a relevant body of knowledge and category of people (social scientists) who may contribute to its solution. They must be influential enough to be able to persuade their colleagues to co-operate. Those who are most closely involved must be able to bear the discomfort that will certainly be experienced during some phases of the work.

The Prospect of Consultant Help

A group prefers to resolve its problems without the help of an outside agency if this can be managed. There is, accordingly, always an initial reluctance to the engagement of any sort of outside specialist. While it is hoped that he will be helpful, his employment constitutes an admission that there are imperfections in the organization and that those who man it are unable to remedy these on their own. Sensitivity can be expected to be especially acute when the expertise of the consultant lies in the field of people and relationships, as it is largely for their practical capacities in these matters that managers and administrators are appointed.

The motivation of the consultant will be suspect. Group members try to ascertain if he is after money or prestige and suspect that he will attempt to take over their jobs or their organization.

They fear – with a good deal of justification – that a change in the internal power structure will ensue if work is undertaken with a social consultant.

Once the consultant is engaged, some interest is vested in his failure, since this would imply that the problem is so intractable that the group cannot be criticized for having failed to cope with it. The consultant's failure would also give objective support to the group's original reluctance to call in outside help and strengthen disinclination to do so in the future.

The social consultant has prestige with the group because of his expertise. But he constitutes a threat and his presence is inevitably resented. It is feared that he will judge the leaders of the group by 'professional' standards rather than by those of everyday organizational life, that he will expect too much from them, will expose their deficiencies by direct statement or by demonstrating his own standards of competence, or will shame them for letting emotional or irrational factors govern their behaviour.

Early Consultations

Early consultations will be occupied largely with examination of the character of the problems to be worked on and the relevance of the consultant's qualifications to these. Group members must know in what areas he professes an expertise, where his competence ends, what can realistically be expected from interaction with him, and what they will themselves have to do. They need some idea of costs, both in money paid to him and in the amount of senior managerial time required on their own side. Arrangements must be made for withdrawal of either side if the relationship is found unproductive.

The group characteristically expect diagnosis of their problems in terms of persons, i.e. judgements of who is right and wrong, who should be encouraged or discouraged. They are greatly relieved if this is not the consultant's approach, though they find his emphasis on matters of relationship, structure, and culture difficult to understand. On the other hand, they will naturally be disappointed if he does not support action in connection with particular individuals where this is what is indicated.

At an early stage a decision will have to be made between the group and the consultant about who his client is, and whether the stated person or persons are the most appropriate. If he has been brought in by an individual, the question may well arise whether that individual had a right to do so: he may not be the leader or representative of the appropriate group; there may be some other person with whom those functions are shared. If so, the latter must also be involved There is often a superior executive committee or a functionally significant representative committee whose sanction it is necessary to seek for the work envisaged. Where this is the case their formal assent to the relationship with the consultant must be obtained and made manifest to the key members of the organization involved, and a means should be created for keeping them in touch with the progress of the work. This is especially important as the consultant's work can rarely be closely localized and often ramifies in unexpected directions. Again, it is quite possible that the personnel in the key operational roles will change: they will be at a loss to know how to behave towards the consultant if the larger institution has not provided guidance through its sanctioning body.

The consultant needs an accepted institutionalized relationship with an individual to whom, by virtue of his office, his main responsibility is recognized to lie, and a formal channel of communication must be established between them. The person to whom he reports should be in a central administrative position, because it is that person, more than any other with whom he is in active contact, who represents the organization to the outside world and carries responsibility for integrating the work of individuals in the group. During periods of stress or uncertainty the leader of the group will have to consider more seriously than anyone else whether to continue the relationship with the consultant. He has to look at this from the viewpoint of the whole group as well as of his own personal feelings.

Where productive changes are unlikely to occur without the collaboration of the other key individuals and their chief executive, the consultant needs at least some situations in which he can work with them as a collective entity.

Looking over the Consultant

The group watch the consultant carefully to see if he attempts a diagnosis before he has really grasped the nature of the problem, made a preliminary assessment of the capacities of the group, and absorbed the atmosphere of their interaction. They will be impatient with the range of the data he seeks and try to tempt him into a superficial diagnosis that avoids the main issues; at one level they will be relieved if he accepts this, but at another, probably more fundamental, level they will realize that he is going into collusion with them to avoid their real problems and is therefore unlikely to be helpful to them. Informally and spontaneously they test whether he violates the confidence of personal communications.

The group are concerned to assess the security of the consultant as a person and as a professional worker. If he is uncertain of himself or his competence, this is quickly communicated to them. They need reassurance that he has been through similar exercises before and that he is not so preoccupied with his personal affairs or his professional career that he is unable to give their affairs his full attention.

They feel reassured if he has a group of professional colleagues. Though they may feel discomfort about being discussed, they like to know that their consultant can himself rely on outside advice, and that if he is absent for one reason or another his colleagues will have sufficient knowledge of their affairs to make some sort of continuity possible.

Though the group are rarely equipped to judge the consultant's theoretical qualifications, his capacity to maintain an independence of judgement and to tolerate strain is evident from his social behaviour, which is therefore assessed with special care in the early consultations.

The first phases of the work are often dominated by the need of the group to 'test out' the investigator as a 'professional' and as a person. The unwitting purpose of their behaviour is to satisfy themselves on his integrity in the role that they and he are together shaping, and to check that he is genuinely involved in making his professional and personal resources available to them.

Looking over the Group

The consultant looks over the group in an assessment of the possibilities of the situation.

He needs to know if the group have sufficient external sanction from the organization as a whole to deal with the stated problems and enlist his help with these; if they hold a sufficient internal warrant in the form of agreement among key members or the right of the leader to employ him; if they include the necessary people and resources for an attempt to deal with the problem; if they have a sufficient measure or potentiality of internal cohesion to permit a constructive approach to their problems and to him; if they can understand the nature and limitation of his competence.

The Main Work Phase

Whatever the consultant says or does when he begins his work, the group hope for magical or painless solutions from him. When he is unable to solve a problem in a single session or at the wave of a wand they feel thwarted and let down. At the same time, this reassures them that he is also human.

They assume that the consultant will do things for them and relieve them of burdens. Instead, they find that they have to continue to carry the main burden themselves – and the burden may seem more onerous than it would have been without him.

The group exert pressure on the consultant to be their executive leader rather than their adviser, to tell them what to do and how to do it.

They become annoyed and hurt when he shows current problems to be related to their own behaviour. This confronts them with the painful necessity of changing themselves and of accepting responsibility for what happens around them. But again it carries a certain reassuring quality as it suggests that he believes they are capable of accepting discomforting communications and have the ability and flexibility to do something about them. They can see that he would not bother to make a diagnosis or give advice if he thought they lacked the resources to act.

When the consultant has shown the usefulness of his work a certain elation develops around him; he and his competence are idealized. Members of the group seek to identify themselves with him. They may well neglect their business tasks in a misguided attempt to preoccupy themselves with the same issues.

If their perspectives are not restored, their own tasks suffer. Alongside the positive elements in their motivation for behaving in this way goes a certain aggression. Their behaviour carries a threatening communication to the consultant of somewhat the following character: 'Since you emphasize the importance of people, relationships, etc., we will abandon other tasks and concentrate on these. The negative consequences of this will be felt in our affairs and you and your advice will be to blame.'

Group members fear that they may become too dependent on the consultant or that, having become dependent, they will not be in a position to disengage themselves from him. To the extent that they do become dependent on him they will resent this and feel bound by it.

At various points in the project the consultant is sounded out on the possibility of his joining the organization instead of operating from the outside. This can represent a recognition of the value of his work and a realistic appraisal of the greater contribution he would be able to make if he were on the premises more continuously, could be given an even more privileged position in the sharing of information, and could concentrate exclusively on the needs of his own employers only. On the other hand, there is often included in these approaches an anxiety lest the consultant should depart before his task is complete, and a wish to reduce the potency of his advice by including him in a hierarchy where he will himself be dependent and will be only one of a number of persons whose advice must be given equal weight in reaching decisions.

At some stages the group members defend themselves against over-dependence on the consultant by withholding necessary knowledge from him. In this way they can reassure themselves that at least they know the local situation better and can insure themselves against his 'omnipotence'.

They hope he will open communication channels, but fear that if he does this will bring unwelcome information. When he does open communication channels among members of the group, or between themselves and other groups, the threat constituted by his presence increases because the first communications are usually of the unfavourable hostile type normally kept out of formal channels; and the possession of the additional information places fresh responsibility on the group. He is accused of complicating issues and of creating the problems he has revealed.

His behaviour with the group at the time of his first major reporting back to them is crucial to the project. Is he merely going to comfort them with a diagnosis and leave them to it, or is he going to be willing to consider alternative solutions with them and help them actively towards them?

When the group are in a phase of doubt or depression about their capacity to make the changes they purport to want, the consultant becomes a target for aggression. He is accused of being hostile towards the group, over-critical, unhelpful, ignorant of the full facts of the case, insufficiently appreciative of the situation of the group, unrealistic, academic, and of not having his feet on the ground. This discharges tension for the group and serves to avoid internal dissension.

The consultant must take a moderate, reality-based standpoint through the oscillations that attend his work. It is necessary to bring the group back both from the fantasy of overnight magical solutions and from fears that the problem is insoluble and nothing can be done. He must encourage a business-like interest in getting the job done, if necessary on a compromise basis. He may be able to help the group to learn from their exaggerated hopes and fears of him how these are endemic in their own leader-follower, executive-adviser, colleague-colleague relationships.

The amount and level of contact between the consultant and the group will vary through time in accordance not only with the needs of the situation but also with the capacity of the people concerned to tolerate the stress in their relationship.

Once the relationship is established the group learn to accept the capacities – and the limitations – of the consultant. They learn to tolerate the mistakes that the consultant will make. They may even be helped by these reminders that he can also err. He comes to be regarded less as a focus of curiosity and excitement, and more as a special sort of colleague with a role complementary to their own.

However much he helps them, interaction with the consultant must constitute a strain for the group. His presence reminds them that they need him. More than this, the consultant is usually able to call their attention to possibilities of achieving higher standards even when they have solved the original problem for which he was called in. This is because it is his profession (and often his vocation) to see new possibilities in established situations and to stimulate change, and because, so far as is known, limits are never reached in the use of human resources. However 'well' a group may be doing, there is always more that they could do.

The group use the consultant as a mirror to assess the magnitude of the changes they have made during the period of their acquaintance with him. At some stages the group or particular members feel that they are not acting as agreed or promised, and avoid contact with the consultant as much as they can.

Relations with Individuals

Individuals within the group will be unevenly committed to the relationship with the consultant. Some will have pressed for his help, others will have been ordered to work with him and will resent him or be indifferent to him. Some individuals infer (sometimes correctly) that he was brought in to strengthen the leadership or some faction against them. They require reassurance that the consultant is looking at the problem as a whole and is concerned with the best solution for all.

Individuals seek constantly to get the consultant to understand the reasons for their publicly expressed 'line', to share their viewpoints (where these are different from those of other members of the group), and to ally himself with them against the rest of the group. They constantly test the extent to which he is prepared to be drawn out of his independent role or to violate personal confidences.

They tempt him to generalizations about society, life, and personality, in attempts to ascertain the limits of his confidence and professional skill.

They seek to get to know him as a person, and make attempts to form private relationships with him and to ascertain his separability from his expertise – as if this will make it easier for them to acquire the latter.

Individuals put pressure on the consultant to give them his impressions of themselves (and of other members of the group) and to make interpretations of the meaning of their behaviour. In order to cope with this he must distinguish between his role and that of an individual therapist, but show his willingness to refer his respondent to a professional therapist if this is really required. In so far as he accedes to the request to supply personal therapy he creates difficulties for himself and for his objectives, diverts attention from objective external tasks, conveys a communication to the group that he sees problem situations in terms of the characteristics of individuals, and reduces their confidence in the other areas of his competence. He will need to show that his refusal of personal therapy is consistent with his obligations to the group – that he can be more useful to them in other ways.

His refusal can take a number of forms. The most oblique – and most effective – method, when individual difficulties are taken up with him as if he is a potential therapist, may be to respond with some indication of his own personal idiosyncrasies. This makes possible a reciprocal identification at a person-to-person level that discourages the further production of personal communications of the sort best made to an individual therapist.

The work of the consultant poses problems for him in terms of the interests of particular individuals as against those of the group as a whole. These are not necessarily the same. From time to time, he finds himself using his influence in the interests of one or another individual, or in the interests of compromises which may not be viable. A partial way out of this dilemma is to arrange that, in addition to a group relationship and a relationship with the chief executive, he will carry certain separate relationships with particular individuals. Another solution is to arrange for colleagues to handle the individual relationships.

Whatever arrangements are made, it is necessary for him to give absolute priority to the needs of the organization, to serve its overall interests, and contribute to its primary task. (In the Davidson case the project was complicated by the existence of two clients – a family system and a business – with contradictory primary tasks.)

The Concluding Phase

When the time approaches for the consultant to withdraw from the relationship or reduce his participation, two tendencies will compete in the group he has been advising. One is an overvaluation of his contribution, coupled with an idealization of him as a hero without whose presence nothing could have been accomplished. The other is to denigrate him and his contribution. Both tendencies threaten the continuation of what has been started. Unless the consultant and the group can steer a course between these extreme viewpoints, there exists a danger that further development will be inhibited by a regression to a position of hopelessness.

The group will find it difficult to persist with the tasks they have set themselves with the consultant. If they are to succeed, he must leave a substantial residue of training in what is relevant to a human problem and in what to expect as a matter of course when a group have embarked on a series of changes. His work will have defeated its own purposes if he has acquired a vested interest in the incapacities of the organization and made himself indispensable.

II. METHODS OF WORK AND THEIR IMPLICATIONS FOR THE SOCIAL CONSULTANT

General Character

The general nature of the investigator's day-to-day techniques of work is determined by the fact that he tries both to understand the situation with which he is confronted and to share that understanding in a way that will contribute towards his respondents' capacity to reach realistic decisions and execute them.

It follows from this (i) that an overall appreciation, however approximate, usually has to take precedence over precise description or measurement of partial aspects of situations; (ii) that the investigator has to acquire a knowledge of the concrete, objective, 'external' environment in which his respondents are operating; (iii) that he has to establish an understanding of the key people involved and of the dynamics of their interrelation, so that he can estimate what it is possible and impossible for them to do – whether or not he thinks he or other people could do more; (iv) that he must keep in particularly close contact with the individual or group directing the organization (or that part of it that he is working with), in order to create situations in which their understanding will grow in parallel with his own.

While the precise techniques of the research worker will vary with individual predilection and personality as well as with the nature of the problems studied, collaborative investigators usually make considerable use of forms of individual interview and group meetings in which attempts are made to facilitate as free a discussion as possible. This is especially the case during the early phases of the work that are concentrated on gaining information.

Individual Interviews

In individual interviews the research worker is concerned to appreciate both the overt, factual content of what is said and the covert content of what is being conveyed. The interview is designed to throw light on complex attitudes and motivations including their unconscious components. This does not mean that respondents are actively encouraged or probed to reveal hidden motives. The depth of such interviews resides less in the respondent than in the interviewer, in the capacity of the latter to infer rather than the preparedness of the former to 'reveal' or 'imply'. It is fatal to the interview if the interviewer tries to make the respondent 'dig' into his feelings. It is less important for the interviewer to probe than to be able to facilitate communication by the respondent, to listen to him, and to understand what he is saying.

Group Discussions

Group discussions are a necessary complement to individual interviews. Differences in viewpoint lead to the elaboration, amplification, and justification of individual opinions, to argument and counter-argument, all of which have both an overt and a covert (or unconscious) content relevant to the research.

In a group situation the investigator is better able to obtain a rounded description of the relevant facts, including such 'subjective' facts as the varying definitions of the situation by individual members of the group and the extent of group consensus or disagreement. He can inform himself about the norms of inter-colleague behaviour, the paths along which power, influence, and authority are exercised and respect accorded. In the group situation it is possible for him to identify factors which might escape him in individual interviews, where his glimpse may be more fleeting or fragmentary. The half-expressed idea of one member may be taken up by others and elaborated. The investigator is able to observe interaction at first hand while members work on the problems they have raised or respond to his questions and observations.

Perhaps most important, so far as the therapeutic component of the work is concerned, is the fact that group meetings in which feelings can be freely expressed are an effective means for developing cohesion and capacity for effective action among members.

In the group discussions the investigator not only collects

the 'objective' facts of the situation as fully as he can but helps the group to voice previously unrecognized or unspoken difficulties. They may discuss matters which are normally considered taboo among themselves but which in fact may have operated to inhibit achievement levels. He encourages them to realize that knowledge of the way they feel about the problems confronting them can become part of their capital for dealing with such problems. He works on the principle that when ideas are allowed to flow freely consecutive ideas will be linked together by a meaning. He may not see the meaning at once – or ever – but there is one to be found.

In both the interview and the group discussion the research worker must accept the fact that the nature of the relationship he forms with his respondent is a major factor in what is communicated to him The character of this relationship must be well understood and borne in mind in the interpretation of data. Understanding the character of this relationship is very much aided and increased through observation by a colleague as well as by the consultant himself.

Earlier work of the type described often took up more directly with respondents the subject of their feelings towards each other and towards the investigator. Because of differences in the nature of problems presented and in agreed terms of reference, present methods used by members of Tavistock Institute tend to focus rather more on the 'objective' tasks of the commissioning group and rather less on the explication of internal group processes, though it is often found essential to retain the right to perform the latter type of task if the occasion requires this. Although the investigator helps the group to voice and discuss feelings and relationships, he makes it clear that explication of the dynamics of their interaction should not be the primary focus of his attention or theirs – since the joint task on which they are engaged is one of improving the functioning of the organization and is distinct from group therapy or group relations training. He helps the group to take into account existing feelings in the same way as they would take into account other classes of fact, to tolerate stress, and to take a long-term view of personal ups and downs. He would be failing in his duty if he substituted for the research and advisory contribution to practical problems a greater preoccupation with personal relations than is necessary for the success of his assignment. On the other hand, occasions arise from time to time where the commissioning group may be at risk in the pursuit of their objectives if they neglect the explication of their own underlying processes and feelings. Here the consultant would be failing in his responsibilities if he did not help with that explication.

Since the investigator is more than a passive recipient of information, there are many occasions on which he reports information back to individuals and groups. Such occasions begin to arise almost immediately because his respondents are anxious to know as soon as possible what he thinks of them and of their capacity to cope with their problems. These communications stimulate elaborations, qualifications, and differences of opinion, which further contribute to his knowledge of the facts of the situation and the way people feel about it. If the investigator is to complete his dual task he is obliged to work with the groups concerned over a protracted period until he can be sure that there is sufficient consensus about the validity or implications of his observations to permit the organization to go forward.

Direct Observation

It is usually essential to supplement interviews and group meetings with direct study of relevant parts of the organization and of relations between them. These parts may consist of executive and advisory divisions, of production and sales departments, of central administrative committees and front-line staff. In this work the investigator adopts an open observational role, after having been introduced by the sponsoring body with a full explanation of his objectives and methods, and the ways in which co-operation is sought. The work is made easier if the investigator is prepared to clarify his role with those observed, and to discuss his observations with them, so that they can contribute their own comments and benefit from his way of looking at social situations.

It is often advantageous to make detailed studies of a few of the key roles relevant to the problems under study. These cover the content of work, the duties of the occupant of the role, the obligations of others towards him, the relationships he carries with superiors, colleagues, and subordinates, the social and psychological atmosphere and pressures in and around the role, the opportunities it confers for satisfaction, and the frustrations and difficulties which the man in question is required to tolerate. By this means the investigator learns about the way the organization functions, and is provided with more material for bringing discussions back from the realms of the abstract or imagined to daily practical realities.

Participation in Operations

As a social scientist, the investigator may originally have been invited into the organization to help with some operation such as selection or training, or requests to do so may be made while he is at work with the organization. Frequently, experimental changes emerge from his work with the organization and he is asked to assist in their design, conduct, or evaluation.

His involvement in these events – whether as observer, adviser, or active participant – provides him with a further set of opportunities to observe the organization at work upon a task; he is able to integrate this information with the rest of his knowledge, and has more to feed back to the organizations on the way they function and on the probable consequences of actions they contemplate.

Implications for the Social Consultant[1]

The consultant needs a basic theoretical training that should have supplied him with an overall frame of reference on society, its institutions, and its associations; with concepts and propositions about kinship, religion, work, recreational and convivial social categories, about formal organizations and informal groupings of various sizes and the relationship of individuals with them; with some understanding of regularities of

[1] The remarks which follow concern ideal desiderata for the training, qualifications, and characteristics of persons engaged in social consultancy. Anyone actually like this would be superhuman.

social process, and of the values, philosophies, and ideas that attend those processes.

He should be familiar with the history, procedures, and findings of the studies conducted during this century of industrial firms, hospitals, schools, and public agencies, and have assimilated their implications.

In addition to training in a social science which takes organizational behaviour as part of its subject matter (sociology, social anthropology, or social psychology), he should have a grasp of one of the sciences dealing with individual personality and also with the pathology of behaviour (psychiatry, clinical psychology, or psycho-analysis). These can further understanding of universal emotional components of behaviour, and of the feelings engendered in individuals and groups in the daily press of life.

The phenomena under study are unlikely to be subsumed under one specialized academic category, and there will be a permanent need to understand the relation arising between the types of force – structural, cultural, or personal factors – operating in the situation studied.

The social science disciplines must be to some extent 'mixed' within the person. When at work the investigator is basically a *person* who, in Rickman's (1951) words, 'at the moment of his most creative endeavours lets these disciplines sink into the background of his consciousness and senses the direction of a process or the degree of freedom of movement in the organization or persons seeking his advice'. Like other professionals he first immerses himself in the situation, and applies the main weight of his formal analysis subsequently. He is able to come back to the basic disciplines only when later mulling over the material. When actively dealing with respondents it is fatal to be thinking: What principle is there in sociology or psychology that could be applicable here?

The social consultant is considerably helped if one of the sciences in which he has been trained has a research tradition that includes first-hand contact with individuals and groups. He should be trained in the systematic collection and evaluation of field data, so that he can know the relative and complementary yields of various types of interview, questionnaire, group discussion, and observation, when applied to specific types of research objective.

The social consultant needs to be the sort of social scientist who gains a genuine satisfaction in working with respondents at first hand, who has a highly developed taste for field work and a sophisticated understanding of his relations with respondents.

His respondents will not co-operate with him unless they feel him to be genuinely interested in trying to understand their situation and to help them. Their conviction will not rest for long on objective qualifications, recommendations from others, or the words he speaks. Practical people trust neither science nor scientists as such, but put their faith in the person. On every project he has to earn the right to do his work, and in each case he does so as a whole person.

He must be able to project himself well enough into the situation of the group concerned to see the situation from their point of view. Yet for their sake as well as his own, he must retain an objective impartiality of judgement side by side with his appreciation of their viewpoints and with a sympathetic identification with their objectives.

The research worker takes for granted that his presence will affect the field of study. He attempts to assess the nature and extent of the disturbance as an aid to the understanding of the problems. He accepts the disturbance as a source of data (often highly significant data) likely to throw light on the substantive problems under study, asking himself exactly why and how the particular disturbance in each particular case occurred in quite the way it did.

He must be sensitive to the contribution he makes, as well as to that made by others, in his reciprocal relationships with them. He should for instance know what makes him anxious, how he usually protects himself from anxiety, how he reacts towards those who have or lack authority, and how much waiting and lack of structure he can endure. He should know in what direction his biases tend.

He should be sufficiently aware of his own emotions to use them in part as data, i.e. to convert what would often otherwise be the deficit of his unacknowledged biases into the capital of known material about the situations in which he becomes involved. He should be able to 'read off' in his own reactions some of the things that are happening in the process he is examining. Rather than be a victim of uncontrollable projective distortion, he should be the beneficiary of a sympathetic identification which he can allow for and use. If he does become anxious – as he will – but can handle and evaluate this, and make the right inferences about events in the group from the fact that he feels anxious, this information can illuminate important events in the structure he is examining. If the investigator knows these limitations and uses the possibilities of being a research instrument, there is every hope that he can derive fruitful hypotheses from his work that will allow other investigators with different (though also known) idiosyncrasies to check his observations against their own.

The foregoing remarks about ideal desiderata in field ability are probably applicable to all successful field workers, whether their objectives are purely academic or combine the academic with the practical. But, because of the special character of the work described in this book, they have special force for the social consultant. This follows from the particular components that enter where respondents are given a reasonable expectation that they are to benefit from what is done.

Because the consultant carries this responsibility, he must be able to anticipate and tolerate the excessive hopes, the excessive disappointments, and the hostility, that will from time to time be connected with his efforts, and to distinguish to what extent these are attached to his role and to what extent to his own particular way of performing it.

The obligations he assumes to the group include that of discussing the contents and implications of the facts and opinions he reports back to them. He has to be able to deal with the emotions which arise on that account, taking into consideration the group's feelings about their situation, the need to get their tasks done better, and the need to present an accurate report.

The social consultant has to be able to tolerate considerable personal strain, not present in the same degree where the operational-advisory component is absent.

One source of strain derives from the volume and the character of communications which come his way. Within a short time the consultant is in possession of many facts, opinions, and sentiments, which the group as a whole has not previously confided to an outside person, and which in many cases individuals in the group have not confided to each other. He has to maintain a relationship with the group and the individual members, in which he and they know that he has knowledge which one person or another is most anxious to possess but which it is not the consultant's function to communicate. At its simplest, this knowledge might be the opinion held by a superior of a subordinate; at a more complex level, it may be his private estimates of their relationships, their individual personalities, and the likelihood that these will change in one way or another. For the sake of his work and for the sake of his respondents considered as a group, he will probably have to withhold much of his appreciation from them, or make it available only partially or from time to time as he thinks opportune. At the same time as he withholds information and opinions that his respondents are anxious to obtain, he does two things with this information which – though known to occur and known to be in the interests of his respondents – make them uneasy and induce feelings of guilt in himself: that is, from time to time he adopts a 'relativistic' attitude to his information on their behaviour that would, in an ordinary context, seem to go with cynicism and indifference; and shares it with his colleagues in a way which, outside a professional setting, would amount to gossip.

A second source of strain derives from the underdeveloped character of social science: the consultant is not in a position to appreciate and anticipate more than a fraction of the complex processes in social situations. The fact that he, trained in social science, is probably in a position to make a slightly better analysis of a situation than his respondents is some comfort to him, but only some, when he is striving to understand, predict, and help.

A third source of strain stems from the fact that in any real situation it is necessary simultaneously to consider multiple categories of data – economic, sociological, psychological, medical, and so on. Since the consultant cannot be equally well equipped in all of these – and cannot always have quick enough access to technical help – he has to tolerate his own relative ignorance outside his areas of greatest competence.

A fourth source of strain is the consultant's knowledge of his own variability as a research or therapeutic instrument. Any experienced social consultant (and indeed any observant field worker) notices the unevenness of his own insight. He congratulates himself one day on what he has recognized, only to feel ashamed the next when he has missed something which he himself in another mood, or another social scientist, would have found quite clear.

A fifth and interlinked source of strain arises from the responsibility taken by the consultant for the fate of the enterprise and of the individuals with whom he is working. Once he undertakes to help them to study their problems, or to make up their minds on how to act, he shares a measure of their preoccupations and anxieties. But there is more to it than this, because he comes with an expertise probably less developed than their own, yet has been brought in with exaggerated expectations of the weight of his contributions. He is inevitably depended on for something that surpasses organizational efficiency and economic benefit, i.e. for an understanding, tolerance, and influence, that will contribute to personal and institutional mental health. While his responsibilities in these respects are more diffuse than those of the medical therapist, their breadth and pervasiveness render them no less strenuous.

The requirements I have mentioned for the individual investigator – theoretical training, an interdisciplinary approach, practical ability to work with others and consciousness of the processes entailed, self-control, self-insight, capacity to tolerate stress – will inevitably be met unevenly in any one person. He will be relatively strong in some of these areas, weak in others.

On any of his projects he will go through phases in which his perceptions will be blocked by his own feelings. The situation under study will sometimes be too complicated for one person to understand.

For these reasons, investigators working on the model

described find it highly advisable to work from a technical base consisting of colleagues who have shared complementary skills, culture, philosophy, objectives, and experience. In the words of W. R. Bion, 'It takes a group to understand a group'.

III. PREPARATION OF THE SOCIAL CONSULTANT

It will be clear from the preceding sections that I consider social consultancy to be a distinct field of work for those social scientists whose interests, aptitudes, and opportunities lead them in that direction, and that I consider that it is possible for it to emerge as a useful profession directly based on the social sciences.

It would clearly be impossible for me to express an unbiased or objective view on this topic. First, it would be unpalatable to admit the possibility that one's long period of training had been irrelevant to one's central tasks. Second, any scientific or professional training merges with the self over years of experience so that it becomes impossible to distinguish what one has been especially trained to do from what one would have spontaneously done in any case.

It should be appreciated also that, in many of the incidents described, an 'objective' outside person, whether or not trained in social theory and research techniques, would have arrived at least at the same diagnosis of the situation, and seen the direction in which the organization should move. On the other hand, I believe that, although his judgement would often be as good as that of the 'trained' person and sometimes superior, the consistency in judgement of the trained person over a protracted period, i.e. his total diagnostic and prognostic contribution, would be greater. Also, I believe that it would be very much more difficult for the untrained person to remain long enough in the right sort of relationship with the organization to enable its members to move appreciably towards the new goals that have been agreed.

On the assumption that social consultancy can become a profession within social science, practised full-time by some social scientists and alongside other work by others, training for it becomes the question of what preparation a potential practitioner should receive alongside his basic training.[1]

A strong argument can be made in favour of postponing any specialized training until after the completion of a first degree in sociology, psychology, or anthropology. Without a minimum period of three or four years of concentrated intellectual preparation in one of these fields – it hardly matters which – it is difficult to see how the individual can become habituated to the systematic thinking and inquiring about social phenomena without which even a rich practical experience and practical intuition can prove idle. After the completion of a first degree there should be a sustained period of field work – whether academic or action-oriented in objective – during which the trainee would work under academic supervision on a research project requiring him to review a theoretical area, define a problem, collect material relevant to it, and argue from pre-existing knowledge and new facts towards a conclusion.

Up to this stage there would be little or no difference between training for social consultancy and the accepted training for social research workers. At this phase, however, it would seem desirable to spend some time in a clinical organization – mental hospital or out-patient clinic – for observation or supervised experience of diagnosis, prognosis, and psychotherapy, in connection with mentally disturbed individuals and groups. Diagnosis and psychotherapy of the mentally ill involve today a meticulous elucidation of the behaviour of the ill person, and of transactions between the therapist and the ill person, that differs in degree from any other social process with

[1] This is, of course, a separate question from the training of the small number of people in Britain who are undertaking social consultancy today as the main, or an important, part of their total work. Some of these have covered ground much like that which I have described as desirable, though not necessarily in that order or in the order that would have benefited them most. Others (like myself) have missed one important element in the training, in the form of work in a clinic or mental hospital. Some of the leaders in this field have come to it from medicine, usually via psychiatry or psycho-analysis. It is to be hoped that more will follow the same path, because of the special knowledge contributed by psychiatry and psycho-analysis, and because of the relevance for this new occupation of professional experience involving responsibility for the fate of others coupled with responsibility to colleagues and a wider society. But for most people, in the future as in the past, this would represent a change of career, and it is more likely that those who decide on part- or full-time social consultancy will start from the social sciences.

which the non-therapist normally comes into contact. Experience of psychotherapy would make the study of 'normal behaviour' more meaningful to the trainee, by exposing him to the exaggerations and extensions of fantasy into action that we label mental illness, and to the dynamic interplay of past and present, imagination and reality, conscious and unconscious, in mental functioning. He would be helped to learn the amount of stress and disturbance that people can be expected to contain, and the signs that indicate that they need help of one sort or another if they are to function effectively. Apart from the knowledge or insight gained, he should benefit from contact with a therapeutic tradition and with a code of ethical responsibility as yet inadequately developed in the social-psychological sciences, which are manned by research workers rather than professional practitioners.

Among those who undertake social consultancy a body of opinion exists that it is desirable for the potential social consultant himself to be the recipient of psychotherapy during some phase of his preliminary training or during his early professional career. This view is certainly becoming more common with regard to potential candidates in the related profession of psychotherapy. In both cases it can be argued that the practitioner cannot apprehend psychological phenomena fully enough until he has been through prolonged self-examination; that he will have difficulty in handling the dependency of others unless he has himself consciously experienced the ramifications of dependency as an adult; that therapy can increase his self-insight and his self-knowledge, and therefore enable him to understand and master his reactions under stress, to allow for his own biases and predilections, and to empathize more effectively with others. My own belief is that it is extremely difficult for anyone to act effectively as a social consultant unless he has himself had some therapy, but that experience in a mental hospital or clinic reduces part of the difficulty and can provide some sort of alternative. It is, of course, elementary common sense to state that on any one social consultancy project exceptional intellectual power or research ingenuity in the practitioner may outweigh in total impact any deficiencies in self-understanding, empathy, and capacity to tolerate stress. This does not vitiate the argument that experience of psychotherapy can generally be expected to advance the perceptiveness and effectiveness of the social consultant.

The final element in the preparation of the social consultant is, of course, a graduated apprenticeship in social consultancy itself. As in other apprenticeships this involves observing senior colleagues at work and undertaking progressively more responsible projects under their supervision. This is easier to arrange than some other occupational preparations are; because of the research component of the work, a major social consultancy project necessarily involves sub-projects of a predominantly investigatory character, which the new social consultant is adequately equipped to undertake on his own. This enables him to make an independent contribution and to secure his position with the client organization, so that if the occasion arises it is fairly easy for him to discuss the implications of his findings.

CHAPTER 6

PROCESSES OF ORGANIZATIONAL CHANGE

THE object of this chapter is to present in systematic, propositional form certain tentative generalizations about organizational change to which the case studies lead or which they underline. The chapter is therefore relevant to the claim that studies of the type I have described have a contribution to make towards general social theory. Few of the propositions, however, have been wholly derived from the three case studies. They are part of a general stream of reflection and research, and profit from existing knowledge gained elsewhere.

I have selected for emphasis mainly observations that the reader can check against the field data previously reported or against reports provided elsewhere by investigators working by similar methods.

It will be appreciated that the generalizations stated are based on retrospective study and not on the testing of hypotheses formally set up before field investigation and tested in a controlled manner capable of replication. This possibility is rare in all field studies. But the claim made here is that the case studies lead to a deeper understanding of organizational change that can be checked against other intimate experiences with organizations and against new data which may be sought in studies more conventionally (and rigorously) organized and controlled.

REVIEW OF FINDINGS AND CHANGES

It will probably be helpful to begin with a summary of the concrete changes in each case.

In the industrial study, what had been presented at first as a management selection task turned out to be a matter of trying to reconcile family and business interests, and of attempting to move from a 'traditional' mode of organization to a 'rational-legal model'.

Under the new personnel policy that was formulated, future directors would be appointed from among senior managers in the business and would include non-relatives. Management trainees would be appointed in order to improve the quality of entrants, to 'objectify' entry procedures and satisfy directors about the grounds for appointment. If more young members of the family joined the firm they would do so in open competition with management trainees. This would be preceded by vocational counselling. Those who did not enter the firm would be helped in starting some other career.

In execution of this policy, the existing chief accountant, a relative, was offered a candidacy for an alternative post, compensation if he did not secure it, and an opportunity for counselling. He accepted this three-part offer and succeeded in his candidacy for the alternative post. The appointment to the Board of a second relative was deferred, but he was given a senior management appointment, membership of the management committee, and a series of consultations designed to improve his managerial capacity. A new chief accountant and secretary, unrelated to the family, was appointed from outside the company; it was agreed that he would be eligible for Board membership in the future.

A new management structure was worked out which gave more opportunity for non-members of the family to participate in decisions and demonstrate their capacities. A systematic review was made of existing managerial staff and certain training procedures were instituted. Some departmental responsibilities were rearranged. Advice was given to both sides on the issue of the future of a senior executive who was a member of the family.

The study of the research unit arose out of a request to me from the head of the unit and his senior colleagues to study the unit and the service in which it was sited, and report back on ways of improving operations.

The study showed that experimental work in patient care was limited by regulations applicable to the whole hospital. But to secure the conditions they wanted, the unit staff would have to show their appreciation of the hospital's obligations and compromise on the amount of freedom they wanted. The total hospital context had to be assumed as the given environment for their work, and attention should not be diverted from internal tasks to problems posed by the environment. The conduct of research was having a positive effect on morale but was leading to an overvaluation of experiment and change for their own sake. The position of research nurse contained incompatibilities between executive and advisory responsibilities. Difficulty in recruiting experienced clinical research workers, and lack of opportunity for supervised research apprenticeship, had led to a vacuum in the sphere of the physicians and to difficulties between them. Research achievements were likely to be modest.

During the course of the project a certain growth of understanding occurred about the way in which difficulties within the service were being projected onto the external hospital administration, and about the way in which the splitting of research and clinical responsibilities was diverting attention from conflicts which each professional person needed to bear for himself. A lead was required at the most senior level in the better integration of the clinical, research, and nursing services. Arrangements were made for the redistribution of the duties of the research nurse so that the supervisory part of her role was handed to the line administration; she was freed for activities of a more consultative character.

The educational project started with a request from the newly appointed head of the management department of a technical college, who wanted the services of his department studied and improved.

Early field work showed that students took a great deal of trouble with their studies and endured considerable discomfort in the hope that they would advance in their careers. But many lacked the personality qualifications for promotion and pinned too much hope on courses and qualifications. Difficulties were arising from the unconventional approaches of the teaching staff, which were not proving as helpful to the students as had been hoped. Studies of firms showed scepticism about training and about the contribution of the technical college. Contact did not inspire confidence.

A study of the teacher's role showed that it was difficult to teach social science to students with technical backgrounds. A fundamental dilemma arose from the fact that the teacher could meet his formal obligations to the student without meeting the student's real needs. Friction arose with firms because the teachers' diagnoses went beyond their capacities for productive action, and because they seemed to be putting pressure on the firms for wider terms of reference than the firms were prepared to give. Support of the teachers by their superior authorities and by colleagues in other departments was uneven.

As the project went on, the teachers critically reviewed the teaching programme and reduced the courses which offered paper qualifications without developing managerial ability. They improved their techniques of teaching emotionally charged material, made their teaching more practical by the use of project methods, introduced a student counselling service, and improved departmental administration. In relations with firms the department lowered its sights to a more realistic level and developed collaborative methods of conducting training surveys and teaching. Teachers concentrated on the development of close links with a relatively small number of firms. They improved their capacities as applied social scientists through advanced training.

The study drew the County Council's attention to the fact that measures designed to protect the taxpayer's investments could make it extremely difficult for the department to achieve its primary task even when the teachers were functioning at their best. Difficulties were arising in meeting the needs of students and firms; the students' needs were personal rather than academic; the department's industrial 'clients' found it hard to make viable arrangements with the teaching group, as the structure of the college was very much less adaptable and flexible than their own. Liberal interpretation of regulations, growth in staff skills, and the adoption of more modest targets made certain advances possible; but these would be limited.

The critical Nature of these Changes and Reorientation

In all three cases the situation of the group called at the least for radical examination and reconsideration of the organization's tasks and resources, and ways of relating the two. In the first and third cases this was accompanied by equally drastic changes. In the second case the administrative change (in the role of research nurse) was minor, though it had additional importance as an example of what could follow from a sociological analysis; the critical nature of the exercise for the organization rested primarily on the confrontation of the three senior people with the need for a unified directorate and on the explicit communication among all sections of the service of what was happening in the service as a whole.

Effect of Interaction with the Social Consultant

It will be understood that I was in the field with each organization for protracted periods, and that our interaction by its nature and duration affected me to an extent that may well have reduced my objectivity even though it increased my contact with their affairs.

I must also have affected the organizations I was studying, since I became a living part of their social structure. I affected their behaviour, in some instances quite profoundly, and the reader will have to use his own judgement as to the extent to which my generalizations about social change are artifacts of my relationships with my clients.

Different Positions of Groups Studied

The ways in which a group regards, diagnoses, and copes with its policy crises depends of course to some degree on its position in the larger structure of which it forms part. One might usefully distinguish between primary groups which form the directorate of a total organization – such as the Board of the Davidson Company – and primary groups directing the affairs of such part-organizations as the management department of the Helmsley Technical College or the James Division and

Research Unit. The significance of the distinction is sufficient to justify separate treatment in the consideration of certain change processes. But practical experience suggests that the seemingly greater freedom of the directorate of a total organization is largely illusory.

THE IMPETUS TO ORGANIZATIONAL CHANGE

Even in the most stable organization a certain amount of variability occurs over time in internal structure and culture, personnel, supply and market position, techniques, and conceptions. We are, however, concerned here with the more challenging situations which arise when conditions force more drastic deviation upon the organization.

The first question is: How does it come about that organizations seek to make significant alterations in their accustomed modes of procedure? To put the same question another way, how do they become aware that they have a crisis on their hands, that their existing policy has failed or is being challenged, and that a new policy is needed?

Clearly some forces operate to maintain, and others to change, existing approaches. So far as factors internal to itself are concerned, an organization or a group will go on behaving in the established fashion if it maintains a record of success in its primary task as judged by agreed indicators; if its formal structure is one designed largely to protect investments, previously decided policies, and chosen staff; if there is a high degree of stability in its personnel, and if existing personnel are more or less satisfied with each other and with their personal lots; if the formal and informal leaders of the organization are personally conservative in outlook; and if the culture of the organization (its philosophies, ideas, and ideals) places a high value on the conservation of tradition.

There is little doubt that constellations of this type go together. Through a rough and ready process of social selection people who seek security tend to gravitate to organizations where drastic change is unlikely, or where they can rationalize a cautious or defensive personal outlook in terms of the needs or emphasis of their work situation. Indeed, the college study, and to some extent the industrial study, show that an organization has its hardest time when the constellation of conservative person and conservative institutional behaviour is threatened or begins to break up.

So far as forces external to the organization are concerned, existing ways of behaviour will tend to be maintained if the resources coming into the organization (staff, raw materials) maintain a steady state of quantity and quality; if the market for the goods or services it produces is stable; if the techniques or conceptions in the total field in which it operates remain more or less constant; and if the organization's closest competitors do not themselves change radically in size, number, or manner of operation.

Conversely, an organization will be much readier to change if it has only a short history, or a history of limited or uneven success; if its formal structure is designed to take advantage of new market opportunities or new techniques; if it has a high turnover of personnel; if its members are actively dissatisfied with each other, their personal lots, or overall policy; if it has adventurous and flexible leaders, or has recently acquired a new leader who is determined to make a personal reputation by doing something different.

Change may be forced from outside by variations in the availability of materials and men, in markets, techniques, and ideas, and in the fortunes of competitors. As important as environmental catastrophes are new opportunities for expanded operations which cannot be easily taken under existing arrangements; an organization may change radically in these circumstances too.

Theoretically speaking, commercial organizations are explicitly designed to be flexible. They are expected to develop a culture favourable to innovation, exploration, and experimentation. In actual fact it is very easy for their structures to become fossilized and their procedures encrusted with tradition, so that fairly drastic events have to occur before any change. This is one reason why commercial organizations often form new companies to tackle new tasks or variations of old tasks.

The crisis which forces change upon an organization often arises round people or is expressed in terms of people. For example, the new head of the Helmsley management department made an unfavourable evaluation of existing teaching practices and brought his department into some degree of conflict with college colleagues and superiors, with students, and with 'user' firms, before a more effective form of collaboration was achieved. In the case of the Davidson Company, the crisis that arose, around the appointment of a new chief accountant and the problems of executives belonging to the family, was closely related to an increase of competition from foreign countries. In the case of the research unit, distress at the shortage of senior psychiatric research workers, and discomfort arising among the physicians as they worked within the vacuum left by this shortage, reflected the strain on the unit in trying to meet the high expectations placed on it.

Even where there is no catastrophic setback or unfavourable evaluation of the present position, new opportunities bring personnel crises, when it is realized that some individuals or groups are not capable of responding to the new demands, or simply that there are not enough people of the required standard within the organization.

It should be clear that subjective factors play a crucial part in policy change. An organization can drift to its destruction if there are not some influential and self-critical people who can see what is happening and have the capacity to take steps about it.

THE UNITY OF ORGANIZATIONAL CHANGE

Although one or other problem in an organization may be singled out for study or administrative action it is rarely found that such isolation reflects sociological or psychological reality. It is impossible to get below the surface of a problem without facing the fact that the solution of one kind of problem depends on solving some of the others – whether or not the other problems have been recognized at the start. *Although not all problems are equally interconnected, the organization is a social system, i.e. a set of closely interwoven and interdependent activities functionally related to each other. Accordingly, if an attempt is made to deal with one problem without recognition of the larger problem of which it is part, it is virtually certain that the attempt will fail.*

The simplest example of the fallacy of the part-problem is, of course, the tendency to define organizational difficulties in terms of individual personalities. In fact, whatever the limitations of the individual or his capacity to damage the organization, there always remain such questions as how he was allowed to get into his role, why it was structured or operated in such a way that it cannot be contained, why his behaviour affects other people and the organization in the way it does, and what consequences there will be for the organization and its tasks if the problems he poses are handled one way rather than another.

Although we have divided the influences which force change upon organizations into the internal and the external, it is clear that these are often, or usually, interdependent. An organization is always an open system closely dependent, whether in the short or long term, upon its environment. *Every change within the organization will, in greater or lesser degree, affect its capacity to draw upon, and provide for, its environment. Every change in the environment (whether in the supply of the men or materials the organization needs or in the goods and services it provides) will display the internal facets of the organization in an altered light.* Organization and environment permeate each other.

SUSTAINING AND OPPOSING FACTORS IN ORGANIZATIONAL CHANGE

Once a change has been initiated, the innovating group will be influenced to persevere with it if there is continued and visible evidence of its necessity. Further, all tasks generate a momentum of their own; people wish to complete them, even, in some cases, in the face of a quite clear indication that they are less necessary than they were originally thought to be or that other tasks should have priority. Additional momentum comes from the investment of group and personal reputations in the success of the operation. Also, new organizational tasks often follow phases of personal difficulties between colleagues; these supply objective and external activity in which they can sink their differences: the enthusiasm with which the Davidson Board tackled questions of management recruitment and development is a case in point.

In the cases I have described, a further element sustaining the change initiated was, I believe, the relationship with myself. The groups seemed to feel a commitment to me, and to feel that they would be letting me down or making themselves liable to reproaches from me if they did not persevere.

There was, of course, the added factor that I was being used as an index of real or imagined, higher or more moral, standards. For members of the college, I, personally, and, more generally, the Institute which I represented, provided an example of social research behaviour with parts of which they identified themselves very closely; members of the company felt that I was in touch with more efficient and less troubled firms with which they compared themselves unfavourably; while members of the research unit assumed that the internal problems of the Tavistock Institute were better handled than their own. This was perhaps not entirely an artifact of the social consultant-client relationship, or a result of the involvement of the Institute, but an external expression of an internal conflict – they were able to use me as the split-off part of themselves that wanted the new situation or the higher standards.

A similar factor was present with the Davidsons in the moral sphere. They would sometimes test projected behaviour against what they imagined to be my ethical standards or the standards which I was emphasizing as those likely to make their company viable. If I would countenance, or regard as 'fair', a piece of managerial behaviour which could be criticized on grounds of 'welfare' or 'human relations', they were reassured.

An effective group will keep the situation under review so that members can drop their efforts to change, or substitute some other change if a realistic appraisal indicates that this is necessary. A slender line separates this reason for a retreat from the rationalization that things are not so bad or so urgent as originally thought, and that it will be possible to cope under existing arrangements. At the same time it is perfectly rational for the group to decide, after attempting a change, that they lack the capacity to carry it through. Indeed, one of the central features of the Helmsley project was just this sort of progressive (and highly realistic and effective) modification of over-ambitious targets.

Even where the change remains manifestly desirable and possible of attainment, several types of barrier to change still exist within each group. *Like individuals, groups are emotionally tied to their past. They repeat even patently unsuccessful ways of meeting problems.* It seems to be reassuring to stick to one's rituals as if they have a certain magic in themselves to cope with life. The Helmsley group was unusual in the speed with which members realized that the issue of diplomas and certificates was irrelevant to much of what they were attempting with students, though the college and County authorities found this very much more difficult to accept. The Davidson group, by contrast, seemed to me to be slow in shedding parts of its behaviour – such as lingering unduly over breaks in the work day, and opening even minor management decisions to every member of the senior management – though such behaviour was patently opposed in spirit to other attempts that the company was making to modernize itself. With the research unit, the part of outmoded ritual to which the group remained unrealistically attached was the fiction that all the troubles of medical units derive from nursing staff and 'administrators'.

Another set of forces sapping a group's ability to persist in a change comes with the dawning of the realization that if the change is successful the resulting rewards and prestige will be unevenly distributed. An individual's doubts about the worthwhileness or validity of the change may well be reinforced if he sees that it is someone else who is likely to get the credit. Surprises can occur; many of the strengths within groups are hidden until emergencies arise; unexpected leaders are thrown up, and it is not uncommon for the leaders themselves to draw back at least for a time from the Frankenstein monsters they have created. A real change in a group's manner of performing a task is almost certain to alter the power and prestige structure – and this will be to someone's disadvantage.

Paradoxically, the will to carry a change through can be weakened by early success in diagnosis of the problem and in dealing with the first phases of the change. This is because the solution of any one problem always poses another, and both groups and individuals may prefer their existing problems to those that will be posed for them if these are solved. People are often a great deal more comfortable with their current difficulties, however much they complain about them, than they feel they will be with the alternatives, or, when they are confronted with the alternatives, often wish they had their old difficulties back. Another way of looking at this source of doubt is to liken social problems to icebergs; in the early stages of an attempt to change, one can easily be appalled by the realization of how deeply and widely the problem ramifies.

Early findings in the Helmsley case study drew attention forcefully to the fact that, if the teachers were to meet the 'real' career needs of students, they would have to enter into a quasi-therapeutic relation with them and act as personnel consultants to their employers. In the case of the Davidson Company the magnitude of the task of reorganization grew as the directorate looked at each level of management; they realized that, through the years, the standards of competence tolerated had been too low; this was enough to bring any group to a halt. With the research unit it was clear that more, or better, research productivity was needed from the group of physicians, but at the reality level this involved an investment in training and research apprenticeship for existing staff which the senior people felt would completely absorb their own energies. Accordingly, as I saw it, a stalemate or a set of retirals from the field was almost certain to ensue.

Certainly one of the key events that discourage a group attempting to change is the discovery that significant changes can rarely be made merely by persuading other people to act differently. *Sooner or later one must alter that last sacred object, oneself. Whatever has been said before, or acknowledged at the intellectual level, the impact of this depresses and retards the group.* Evidence for this was seen in the change in the Helmsley group, when their attention was forced onto the fact that if their expertise in management was to be trusted by the students they would have to run their department more efficiently; in the reluctance of the Davidson directorate to face the fact that they needed to act more directly and effectively in their departmental responsibilities, rather than confine themselves to attempts to improve recruitment, selection, and appraisal procedures, and to the design of neater management structures and procedures for meetings; and in the negative reaction in the research unit to my communication that if the general body of staff were to be persuaded to integrate their activities better, the top three, currently meeting as a research project committee, would need to remain together in demonstrably effective collaboration.

CHANGE PROCESSES WITHIN THE PRIMARY GROUP

Once a group has established a new policy or new mode of action it enters an excited phase. Members feel exhilarated at being in a position (through their enterprise, authority, or command over resources) to influence their own fate. *They characteristically overvalue novelty and tend to devalue or underrate much that was functional and positive in their past.* We saw this in the over-enthusiasm of the Helmsley department for teaching in unstructured situations and in their low regard for more conventional didactic methods; in the reluctance of the Davidson directorate to trust their own judgement about staff they had known for years, and in their wish to substitute formal evaluation procedures; and in the excitement in the research unit about research and experiment as against the traditions of nursing care.

Beneath or alongside this type of euphoria lies a certain amount of anxiety about the capacity of the group to carry the change through. Despite their negative side, difficulties and obstacles function as an 'explanation' of why people do not do better than they do; they can always take the line that they could achieve remarkable things if only such and such a factor (or person) were not present. When members of a group find themselves in a position to remove such obstacles they risk standing exposed with only themselves to blame in the event of failure and become ambivalent about doing so.

A depressed mood follows early euphoria when the changes that are planned meet the test of reality. Often the plans are over-ambitious. In this case the group must accept the fact that plans have to be scaled down, that they can get something done only if they reconcile themselves to how little they can really do, that perfectionism is equivalent to defeatism and omnipotence to impotence. Most salutary of all, as previously indicated, is the realization that other people cannot be left to make all the changes, that the group and the individual members must themselves change.

At this stage doubts are manifested about the worthwhileness of the change, about the capacity of the group to carry through the change, and about the capacities of individual members to contribute to the change. Radical and conservative factions are established. Recriminations ensue about the extent of individual and factional identification with the objectives, extent, modes, and pace of the change. Certain individuals within the group will be seized with doubts about their own capacity to contribute and about the likelihood that they will come off well in the change. They will make unwitting attempts to sabotage the change or divert more effective colleagues from their own tasks so that all will be equal.

Gradually more realistic estimates are made of what changes are possible; of what the rest of the organization and the outside world will accept; and of the capacities of the group and the individual members. Some members, including certain of those previously assumed to have most to contribute, are written off with respect to part of the expectations aroused about them. New leaders emerge. *There will be a rearrangement of the internal power and prestige structure, and a release of some human resources contained within the group but not previously available.*

CHANGE PROCESSES IN RELATIONS WITH THE REST OF THE ORGANIZATION

If one group in an organization is initiating changes, the rest of the organization will not watch this unmoved.

Colleagues 'sit pretty' in the sense that though the change might redound to their eventual advantage they do not have to suffer all the discomfort and apprehension of the innovating group. They are not personally committed if the changes are unsuccessful. At the same time, if the changes go well, they will not share the rewards or praise to the same extent as members of the innovating group. They will envy them this possibility.

There will exist some investment among colleagues in the failure of the innovation. Its failure will be an implicit argument for the maintenance of the *status quo* and the folly of improvement. One way in which this ambivalence manifests itself is in the excessive hopes placed by colleagues on even the most modest types of innovation: this guarantees disappointment. If the innovating group has over-admiring, over-expectant colleagues as friends it will not need enemies.

It is tempting in this sort of situation to classify colleagues into those who are friendly and those who are hostile towards the innovation. Though it is true that individual colleagues will vary in their attitude, this clouds the fact that the ambivalence described must exist in every colleague. *The organization undertakes an emotional division of labour in attitudes towards the innovators in just the same way as it distributes any other organizational task.* One person will express an unqualified enthusiasm for the new venture, and another the opposite view, in a way that neither would do without the group insurance provided by the contrasting protagonist. If one person had to bear the whole attitude – taking responsibility for the group – he would have to experience both aspects. If one 'extremist' left the group there would be shifts of opinion among those who remained so that the total range of feeling would still be exhibited.

Whether or not the innovating group is the directorate of the organization, the relationship of that group with colleagues will be uneasy. There occur outbreaks of reciprocal paranoia as well as euphoria.

Where the innovating group is not the directorate of the organization – as in the case of the Helmsley department and the research unit – the directing group will vary in its preparedness to protect the innovators and give them the special conditions they require. This is partly because of the ambivalence already described, but also because of the public responsibility of those in authority. Members of the directorate are held responsible for implementation of policy and deviation from rules; they need to defend themselves against an infinite invasion of their right to legislate and regulate. They have internal responsibilities to persons, other than the innovators, who will be watching them closely to see if the special exceptions made for that group are really essential for the experiments or amount to favouritism and could be extended to include them also. It is in fact extremely difficult for an observer of the directing group to distinguish intransigence from reality-based reasons which the group may have for digging in its heels.

When the innovating group is pessimistic in mood and becomes uncertain about whether it can achieve its aims, it drains off its internal tensions by calling attention to the limitations on its freedom imposed by the members of the directing group, their 'rigidity', 'shortsightedness', 'intolerance', and 'conservatism'; and to the unwillingness of colleagues outside the group to collaborate, and their wish to see the enterprise fail.

All parties will precipitate test cases. These test cases are variously used by all concerned to illustrate those aspects of the total situation that are most favourable to their rationale of the moment. The anxieties of the parties about latent oppositions and unfavourable judgements will precipitate situations that reify those oppositions and judgements.

Where the innovating group is the directorate itself, the group will also have an uneasy relationship with the rest of the organization. Subordinate groups will be worried because of the probability that changes will be imposed on them from above, because they will be in the front line of changes they will not have initiated, and because their 'deficiencies' will be used as explanations for the inability of the directorate to carry through the changes.

SYSTEMS OF DEFENCE

Groups, as well as individuals, possess or create sets of 'defences' – i.e. behaviour, attitudes, theories, and rationalizations that serve to protect them against real or imagined external criticism and against their own anxieties about the success or worthwhileness of what they are doing.

The defences that constitute one form or another of temporary or personal retreat from the field – resignation, illness, late-coming, absence from key meetings, discovery of the greater priority of alternative tasks – are fairly obvious. So is the 'flight into reality' of stressing the negative aspects of the ambivalence of colleagues, and calling into being an opposition that would otherwise remain immanent.

One common defence is the setting of over-ambitious targets. This happened in the early phase of the Helmsley project. It was easy for group members to explain to themselves and to others that they could not succeed because they needed a staff double the size and with much more relevant experience. This was especially provocative for the college and County authorities since they did not feel that they had sanctioned the department's targets.

At the same time the setting of over-ambitious targets serves to avoid the real challenge that all groups have to face, i.e. how to do the best that is possible for them with such resources as they have or can reasonably secure.

Perhaps the research unit may also be said to have been defending itself against failure in achievements that reality made possible by adhering to expectations that had no chance of realization.

The tensions and interpersonal difficulties of the innovating group can lead members to become so preoccupied with internal issues as to 'explain' why they are not succeeding in their tasks.

Over-insistence on the clarification of roles, objectives, and structure can also be substituted for attending to the external task. This was evident in the research unit where the physicians had to be shown that, in a new and fluid group, roles can never be absolutely defined; that within wide limits professional colleagues must find their own level; and that the bandying about of the concepts of role clarity, overlapping authority systems, and so on, served mainly to avoid more real pressing issues. We saw this also in the Davidson case when structural and procedural solutions were often canvassed in situations where simpler, more direct, and more economical executive action was indicated.

A further characteristic defence in the face of fears about adequate achievement is over-democratization. In the Helmsley case too many decisions were taken to total staff meetings, and in the Davidson case too many matters were referred to the whole Board or whole management committee. In the research unit equality of opportunity for research was given to physicians unequal in their capacity to make scientific contributions.

Also, a group will halt itself with exaggerated sensitivity to the welfare of individuals, which would not preoccupy it to the same extent if it were confident of its success in its external, objective tasks. It would press on with the tasks and resign itself to the casualties, or return to pick them up once the battle was over.

These defensive modes of behaviour have an importance beyond the fact that they provide rationalizations for inadequate achievement, for it is only too easy for a group to substitute work on its defences for work on its primary task.

FUNCTIONS OF CONFLICT

Conflicts between individuals and groups are often functional for organizations and productive of positive adaptive changes. Difficulties between the sales and production departments in the Davidson Company had precipitated a decision to install a machine accounting system. This can be viewed as an expensive way of by-passing a management problem that should have been dealt with more directly. Whether or not that was true, the new accounting system brought its own benefits and may well have been justified on its own merits.

The flaring up of conflict displays in extreme terms problems that might otherwise be held at the margin of the organization's attention, such as strains between people and departments, between buyers and suppliers of raw materials, between salesmen and their markets. It impresses upon the directorate the need for change and provides a rationale for drastic action. It provides an opportunity of observing how leading staff tolerate (or fail to tolerate) tensions. It also makes it possible for those staff to learn the levels of their own maturity or long-term management abilities.

Organizational conflict provides an opportunity for the directorate to take responsibility. Indeed, some crises seem to be provoked largely by the need of the members of the organization to test their leadership's capacity to lead. If proper advantage is taken of the situation, the directorate can both provide a reasonable solution of the concrete problem and go about it in such a way as to make an effective communication about the way in which problems should be handled and the ways in which the needs of the organization are balanced against those of individual members.

It would, of course, be wrong to assume that internal conflict and competition are always functional for the organization. Capacity to overcome a rival is, for instance, no criterion of the superiority of the victor's point of view or way of work so far as the operations of the whole organization are concerned. There is no necessary link between ability to get one's way with one's colleagues, and capacity to impress consumers of one's employer's goods and services. It is for this sort of reason that the directorate of the Davidson Company and the research unit could not leave internal personnel affairs to the free play of spontaneous forces.

TRANSITIONS BETWEEN PHASES OF ORGANIZATIONAL DEVELOPMENT

The policies and procedures appropriate at one stage of an organization's history can become dramatically unsuited at another. *Catastrophes occur when the directorate fails to recognize the organization's phase of development or, although it recognizes a change of phase, tries to deal with it through the structure and culture appropriate to an earlier stage.* It can also happen that an organization will miscalculate its phase of development and try to do more than it is yet equipped for. *While the effort to recoup its position subjects the organization to a critical phase of its existence, it is in the experiencing of that critical phase that the organization can rediscover itself.*

In the Davidson case the company's modes of organization and operation had lagged behind the need to operate in a less tradition-bound, more economical, fashion. With increasing external competition, and with the greater rationalization of management selection, development, and appointment in other business firms, the company was likely to drift into increasing business difficulty through reliance on approaches more appropriate to a less competitive age.

The issue with which the Davidsons were faced was wider than that of the restriction of leading roles to family members. The sanctity of tradition in this sphere carried with it a psychological inhibition against any sort of change in established modes of action. If the firm was to survive in its environment the crust of custom had to be broken somewhere.

The Davidsons needed to 'bureaucratize' themselves; to examine the occupants of the leading roles as objectively as possible; to assess their capacity to contribute to the needs of the firm; to reduce the number of passengers; to ensure a flow of the best new talent they could attract; to build up those new management trainees as quickly as possible; to divorce sentimental consideration from merit and qualifications in making appointments and promotions. At the same time they had to do this in a way that would liquidate existing expectations as painlessly as possible, and would mobilize the support of the staff for these changes as conducing to the common long-term interest. They had to manage the change in a way that would vitalize the resources of the organization and not wither them, and help the staff to see new policies and new people as accretions to their strength rather than threats.

On the other hand, members of the Helmsley management department might be said to have been tackling tasks before their own competence had caught up with their enthusiasm, and before students and firms were ready for such advanced work.

The research unit had been set up largely to undertake clinical research, but could not do much immediately. A sustained training programme had first to be undertaken with the physicians, and a scientific culture had to be built that would foster responsibility and collaborative inquiry and experiment.

Just as different procedures are appropriate to the different phases of an organization's affairs, so are different sorts of people. The most obvious reason is technological. A skill in keen demand at one phase may be less important at another; so may be particular types of personality and habits of thinking. We saw this in all three cases – at the point of study, the Helmsley department needed staff willing to judge themselves against the manifested needs of students and firms; the Davidsons needed managers who would act in accordance with more objective and less traditional values than those formerly obtaining, yet would be able to tolerate for some years a continued emphasis on such values in their seniors; the research unit needed members who would devote themselves to the construction of a base for an institution, rather than people burning to turn out research results. And all needed a proportion of staff with an unusual degree of openness of outlook.

DEVIATION BY THE PART-ORGANIZATION

An organization can be bound by its past even when it is a private one, and its fate is in the hands of its own directorate which itself is seeking to change. When the Davidsons shook themselves free of their own past practices as these applied to themselves, they found the pattern which had been imprinted on the rest of the business over the decades difficult to alter.

Transitional difficulties are of course the more acute for the innovating group when it is not itself the directorate, and has the double task of carrying out pioneering work and obtaining conditions within its own larger organization that will make that pioneering possible.

Once it is agreed that a section of an organization may try to change, or develop some new activity, the fundamental questions that need to be asked by the overall directorate are: Under what conditions is its work possible? and How can we create those conditions?, rather than To what extent do we have to change the existing structure to make it possible for the innovating group to do what it wants to do? And it must be clearly understood from the beginning that the conditions needed are unlikely to be known until the experimental phase is under way.

The most viable arrangement is likely to be one in which the directorate is involved with the innovating group in the change on a continuous basis (even if this goes no further than regular reporting back); the innovating group is officially designated a 'research and development unit'; the limits of the experimenting group are clearly defined; maximum protection is given to the innovating group against pressure of current operational needs and against pressure to conform to established practice; and the structure of the innovating part-organization is kept as open as possible until clarification is achieved of the precise outline of its tasks and the way these are likely to be achieved.

If new tasks are to be undertaken, precedence must be given to those tasks rather than to the existing structure in which the innovating organization is located. Unless this is done, everyone has to try to do a new job with a tool designed for an old one. The assumption that the innovating group should attempt to do this is evident from reactions to practical deviations from standard organizational behaviour even when experimentation is nominally sanctioned, but also from the fact that it is rare for organizations to use all the flexibility that they in fact possess. This became clear during the Helmsley study when, in the middle of controversy between the staff and the County authorities about research and consulting facilities and the amount of teaching officially required, we found rulings from the Ministry and County Council showing that it was quite simple to empower the staff to do much of what they wished without drastic changes of regulation.

The difficulty we are discussing – that which arises when an attempt is made to develop new activities in an older, more established structure – naturally becomes additionally complicated when the main part of the impetus to change comes from an innovating group that is not the directorate. The innovators are in the position of claiming a privilege rather than demanding rights.

But even where the impetus has come from the directorate, and the directorate continues to supply sanction and moral support, the innovators remain bound by the premises of institutionalized practice and colleagues' opinion. The right to deviate cannot simply be conferred on them; they have to earn it.

THE NEEDS OF LEADERSHIP DURING CRITICAL CHANGE

In times of critical change it is particularly important (and particularly difficult) for the directorate to look realistically outside and inside the organization, and to relate the two aspects effectively. And that effectiveness must be one that refers to the long term, rather than to a present-day opportunism that will eventually repel consumers or suppliers or sap the values of colleagues and subordinates.

Looking outside, the leadership must be able to judge what the real needs of the present or potential consumers are, and how they can be influenced or anticipated. That judgement often needs to be reinforced by an independent outside assessment.

There is more than one sort of information that the organization needs to have about its environment. One type of information concerns the extent and distribution of the present and potential demands for its goods and services. A second type concerns the dynamics of its relationships with representative consumers – what are the meanings of its product and service in the consumers' life space; how are these meanings handled; which of those consumers' relationships does its product or service mediate; how are the organization, its products, and the intermediaries between it and the public perceived by its consumers and compared with competitive suppliers? *A third type of 'environmental' assessment that must be made is of the extent of correspondence or discrepancy between the image that exists of the organization and the image that seems needed to bind its consumer to it.* Too often organizations mesmerize themselves with the culture that they have developed and become captives of their past. Or they engage in a desperate 'me-too-ism' with their industry or profession – whether or not this is relevant to present-day needs.

It is rarely the case that an objective assessment of the external environment reduces alternative courses of action so drastically that it is self-evident on what the organization should concentrate. This is still a matter of judgement – of how things are likely to go in the outside world, of how competitors are likely to behave, of resources that can be mobilized in the organization, and of the capacity of the organization to develop a product or service that stamps it as distinctive. Through this means, i.e. through realistic and selective concentration, the organization can reduce its dependence on its environment and make at least part of its environment dependent on it. This is unlikely to be achieved unless the environment is kept under constant review – as is evident from the chronic trap of single-shot research into which business organizations fall.

The leaders must be able to tolerate receiving the assessment of their environment and their relations with it. Their capacity to accept the facts of their environment may well fall short of the level necessary if they are to profit fully. Students of organizations are familiar with the anger turned on the research worker or executive who brings unwelcome news, and with the temptation within all but the most resilient organizations to protect themselves against that news or the necessity for change by expelling or ridiculing the bearer. Unfortunately this does not at the same time expel the environmental realities which they recognize.

Looking inward, the leadership is obliged to treat the structure as an instrument planned to do the indicated job or, if necessary, to amend that instrument. No change will succeed unless views on means and ends are widely shared among members of the organization. A course has to be steered between evolving along the lines that those who execute decisions think should be followed and imposing from above a definition of what is needed. In the past decades, emphasis on 'human relations', 'participative leadership', and so on, has perhaps been taken to an extent that suggests an abdication of leadership. It is an irresponsible and eventually an ineffective leadership that fails to communicate its objectives and the means intended to attain these, and that does not invite suggestions. But there is little doubt that organizations function best when leaders lead.

A nice balance has also to be maintained between letting ends determine means and letting existing resources and means determine ends. It is a real demand that must be responded to, bygones must be recognized as bygones, and care must be taken to draw additional resources or develop new procedures if these seem necessary. *But the leadership can start only from where the organization is – if the skills and orientations of the existing staff still have value these must be the fulcrum of new effort.* In the Helmsley case existing staff showed a remarkable capacity to extend their teaching to wider groups and to supplement engineering teaching with down-to-earth organizational advice. In the research unit it seemed prudent to develop research staff rather than to hope for the arrival of someone who would fill the research gap.

The staff must be organized in ways appropriate to the nature of the tasks required, to their environment, and to their own capacities. But the way they are organized expresses more than considerations of efficiency. The administration is more than a technical instrument. It is the clearest communication of the philosophy of the leadership of the enterprise. It tells the staff what the leadership thinks of them, what it thinks of suppliers, what it thinks of customers and how it estimates its own future. Although the staff will not respect a leadership which permits an inefficient organization, they will sabotage one that neglects the needs of its members and they will be indifferent to one that plans only for today.

More widely, the leadership needs to express in its handling of crisis an institutional wisdom rather than opportunistic decision-taking. Such behaviour helps all members to acquire a respect for the purposes and management of the organization, and an understanding of the reasoning behind its policies. This will help them to sustain periods of stress, give them guidance on action when they cannot lean on distinct rules or on senior advice, and enable them to evaluate their behaviour against organization-wide standards.

Knowledge of the external environment must be supplemented by knowledge of the organization's inner resources, more especially its personnel resources. The leadership must know the capacity of key staff members. This includes those whose steadiness and open-mindedness contribute to a collaborative atmosphere for work as well as those who make and execute policy. It should be known who is likely to respond to new opportunities and challenges, and who will be frightened by these. While organizational change provides manifold opportunities for those able to accept them, it simultaneously disturbs those who have gravitated to roles and relations which protect the more vulnerable aspects of their personalities.

The leadership should understand the balance of forces in the internal politics of the organization. This is as potent as technological equipment and skill, and individual abilities, in determining what can and cannot be done.

It is, however, wrong for the leadership to let its policies be determined by the individual talents and idiosyncrasies of the staff or by the politics of the relations between them. These are factors to be weighed, limiting conditions to particular courses of action. If given logical priority over organizational needs, however, they will divert and pervert the more adaptable parts of institutional behaviour and prevent the organization from fulfilling itself.

REFERENCES

Introduction

BARNARD, C. I. (1948). *The functions of the executive.* Cambridge, Mass.: Harvard University Press.

BOWLBY, J., JAQUES, E., KELNAR, J., MENZIES, I. E. P., MORRIS, B. S., SUTHERLAND, J. D., & WILSON, A. T. M. (1947). Social therapy. *J. soc. Issues* **3,** No. 2.

Bull. Menninger Clinic (1946). **10,** No. 3. Topeka, Kansas.

CARTWRIGHT, D. (1958). Some things learned: an evaluative history of the Research Center for Group Dynamics. *J. soc. Issues* supplement series, No. 12.

CARTWRIGHT, D., & ZANDER, A. (Eds.) (1953). *Group dynamics: research and theory.* Evanston, Ill.: Row, Peterson; London: Tavistock Publications.

GIBB, J. R., & LIPPITT, R. (1959). Consulting with groups and organizations. *J. soc. Issues* **15,** No. 2.

JAQUES, E. (1951). *The changing culture of a factory.* London: Tavistock Publications; New York: Dryden Press.

LEWIN, K. (1950). *Field theory in social science.* New York: Harper; London: Tavistock Publications, 1952.

MAYO, E. (1933). *The human problems of an industrial civilization.* New York: Macmillan.

RADCLIFFE-BROWN, A. R. (1940). On social structure. *J. Roy. anthrop. Inst.* **70.**

RICE, A. K. (1958). *Productivity and social organization: the Ahmedabad experiment.* London: Tavistock Publications.

ROETHLISBERGER, F. J., & DICKSON, W. J. (1939). *Management and the worker.* Cambridge, Mass.: Harvard University Press.

SHILS, E. A. (1951). The study of the primary group. In Lerner, D. & Lasswell, H. D. (Ed.), *The policy sciences.* Stanford: Stanford University Press.

SUTHERLAND, J. D. (1946). Social therapy: a trend in social science. *Personnel Mgmt.,* June-July-August.

TAVISTOCK INSTITUTE OF HUMAN RELATIONS (1950). *Development and work, 1946-50.* London: T.I.H.R.

TRIST, E. L. (1957). *The Institute in retrospect and prospect*. London: T.I.H.R.

WILSON, A. T. M. (1955). A note on the social sanctions of social research. *Sociol. Rev.* **3,** No. 1.

Chapter 4

COOK, P. H. (1951). Methods of social research. *Austral. J. Psychol.*, **3,** No. 2.

MCGREGOR, D. (1960). *The human side of enterprise*. New York: McGraw-Hill.

RICKMAN, J. (1951). Methodology and research in psychological pathology. *Brit. J. med. Psychol.* **24,** Part I.

SELZNIK, P. (1957). *Leadership in administration*. Evanston, Ill.: Row, Peterson.

SHILS, E. A. (1959). Social inquiry and the autonomy of the individual. In Lerner, D. (Ed.), *The human meaning of the social sciences*. New York: Meridian Books.

SOFER, C., & HUTTON, G. J. (1958). *New ways in management training*. London: Tavistock Publications.

WILSON, A. T. M. (1948). The therapeutic approach to human problems. *The Seeker*, January-February.

WILSON, A. T. M. (1955). A note on the social sanctions of social research. *Sociol. Rev.* **3,** No. 1.

Chapter 5

BION, W. R. (1948-1950). Experiences in groups I-VI. *Hum. Relat.* **1,** Nos. 3 and 4; **2,** Nos. 1 and 4; **3,** Nos. 1 and 4. Reprinted in *Experiences in groups and other papers*. London: Tavistock Publications; New York: Basic Books, 1961.

BOTT, E. (1957). *Family and social network*. London: Tavistock Publications.

HUGHES, E. C. (1959). The study of occupations. In Merton, R. K., Broom, L., & Cottrell, L. S. (Eds.), *Sociology today*. New York: Basic Books.

JAQUES, E. (1948). Interpretative group discussion as a means of facilitating social change. *Hum. Relat.* **1,** No. 4.

LIPPITT, R., WATSON, J., & WESTLEY, B. (1958). *The dynamics of planned change*. New York: Harcourt, Brace.

RICE, A. K. (1949). The role of the specialist in the community. *Hum. Relat.* **2,** No. 2.

RICKMAN, J. (1951). Methodology and research in psychological pathology. *Brit. J. med. Psychol.* **24,** Part I.

SCHWARTZ, M. & C. G. (1955). Problems in participant observation. *Amer. J. Sociol.* **60,** No. 4.

SOFER, C., & MENZIES, I. E. P. (1960). Opportunities and problems in the study of attitudes. In *Attitude scaling*. London: Market Research Society.

WILSON, A. T. M. (1947). The development of a scientific basis in family casework. *Soc. Work* **4,** No. 3.

ZANDER, A. (1958). Group membership and individual security. *Hum. Relat.* **11,** No. 2.

Chapter 6

EMERY, F. E. (1959). Characteristics of socio-technical systems (cyclostyled). London: T.I.H.R. (Tavistock Publications, in press).

LAZARSFELD, P. F. (1959). Sociological reflections on business: consumers and managers. In Dahl, R. A., Haire, M., & Lazarsfeld, P. F., *Social science research on business: product and potential.* New York: Columbia University Press.

MENZIES, I. E. P. (1960). A case-study in the functioning of social systems as a defence against anxiety. *Hum. Relat.* **13,** No. 2.

RICE, A. K. (1958). *Productivity and social organization: the Ahmedabad experiment*. London: Tavistock Publications.

SELZNIK, P. (1957). *Leadership in administration.* Evanston, Ill.: Row, Peterson.

SOFER, C. (1955). Reactions to administrative change. *Hum. Relat.* **8,** No. 3.

WEBER, M. (1947). *The theory of social and economic organization.* Edited by Parsons, T. London: Hodge.

INDEX